Foreign Language Proficiency in the Classroom and Beyond

Edited by Charles J. James

In conjunction with the American Council
on the Teaching of
Foreign
Languages

National Textbook Company, *Lincolnwood, Illinois U.S.A.*

1988 Printing

Copyright © 1985 by National Textbook Company
4255 West Touhy Avenue
Lincolnwood (Chicago), Illinois 60646-1975 U.S.A.
All rights reserved. No part of this book may
be reproduced, stored in a retrieval system, or
transmitted in any form or by any means, electronic,
mechanical, photocopying, recording or otherwise,
without the prior permission of National Textbook Company.
Manufactured in the United States of America.
Library of Congress Catalog Number: 84-62278

7 8 9 0 ML 9 8 7 6 5 4 3 2

Contents

Foreword

This volume of the ACTFL Foreign Language Education series is, like its predecessor, about language proficiency. The volume is thus unique in the series in that it deliberately follows upon and continues the discussion begun in last year's volume. Now that the profession has outlined what proficiency is, or at least can be, and how the concept of proficiency has developed over the past thirty years, it is the task of this year's volume to make specific, even controversial statements as to what proficiency means for quite diverse groups of practitioners: the classroom teacher, the curriculum developer, the language-learning researcher, the textbook publisher, and the businessperson. As the Introduction emphasizes, it is time to do things with proficiency.

One of the first things that I want to do as editor is to acknowledge the following individuals for contributing to what will prove, we hope, to be a high-level writing sample: the authors, of course; the Advisory Committee (Theodore V. Higgs, Remo Trivelli, Heidi Byrnes, June K. Phillips); Dale L. Lange; C. Edward Scebold; and my wife, Carol. Special thanks go to Robert R. Heitner, Lee B. Jennings, and Heinz C. Christiansen of the University of Illinois at Chicago. Space restrictions do not permit me to detail the extent of your individual contributions. Thank you all very much.

Introduction

Learning from Proficiency: The Unifying Principle

Charles J. James
University of Wisconsin-Madison

There is a saying attributed to the Chinese:

> I hear and forget
> I see and remember
> I do and understand

For over twenty years the foreign language teaching profession in the United States has been hearing a substantial amount from researchers about the nature of language itself and what it means to learn a second language. Under the influence of the more radical forms of audiolingualism, it often ignored what it was hearing from students about language, namely, that while language may be a structured and "drillable" system of human communication, it is also a very flexible and highly individualistic one, used by a variety of personalities for a variety of purposes, both private and public.

For the past ten years the foreign language teaching profession has seen a substantial number of books, newsletters, journal articles, and text material related to what learners should be doing with the language in real and

Charles J. James (Ph.D., University of Minnesota) is Assistant Professor of German at the University of Wisconsin-Madison, where he teaches language and methodology courses. He was coeditor of Volume 4 and editor of Volume 14 of the ACTFL Foreign Language Education Series. His articles have appeared in *Foreign Language Annals, Unterrichtspraxis,* and other journals and anthologies in the United States and the Federal Republic of Germany. He is a member of ACTFL, IFLTA, Gesellschaft für Angewandte Linguistik, TESOL, Phi Delta Kappa, treasurer and member of the Executive Council of the Chicago/Northern Illinois Chapter of the AATG, and national treasurer and member of the Executive Committee of the AAUSC. He is a consultant to language textbook publishers, as well as a reader/referee for *Unterrichtspraxis.* He has been trained in the techniques of the Oral Proficiency Interview at workshops at the Defense Language Institute in Monterey, California, and in conjunction with the Illinois Foreign Language Proficiency Project.

simulated situations. However, only in the past five years can it be said that the profession has begun to focus more clearly on exactly what is required to motivate learners to *do* things with the language and, as a result, retain acquired or learned language skills over a period of time that lasts longer than the time spent in the classroom. We as educators have also begun to deemphasize talk about language and the mechanical demonstration of language behavior in the language class, while emphasizing direct active participation by the learner in the language-learning process.

Opposites and Continua

Our profession is dominated by opposites. Like the search for the Holy Grail with its promise of controlling the uncontrollable and knowing the unknowable (5), most human beings in Western cultures seem to be addicted to simplifying the unsimplifiable; that is, they are addicted to reducing complex processes to binary code. As a result our professional machinery is studded with ON/OFF switches: audiolingual vs. cognitive code learning, internal vs. external motivation, subjective vs. objective testing, continuous vs. noncontinuous measurement, parametric vs. nonparametric statistics, closed vs. open test items, direct vs. indirect evaluation, discrete-point score vs. global rating, audio vs. video media, aural vs. oral channels, true vs. false, active vs. passive, receptive vs. creative, input vs. output, acquisition vs. learning, and now, achievement vs. proficiency. Language, however, is not a binary phenomenon, and language learning and acquisition is not an all-or-nothing proposition to be confirmed by an accumulation of points or a passage through a series of exercises and courses. Proficiency is a continuum, with isolated linguistic items at one end and individualistic language samples at the other, with a variety of combinations in between, their number limited only by the number of people using the language and the kinds of environments in which they operate. A person rated, for example, Novice Mid in speaking, according to the ACTFL Provisional Proficiency Guidelines (1), has demonstrated a level of proficiency that can be described and documented, whether or not a particular lexical item is present, or whether or not a particular structure is used in a certain way. It is admittedly possible to define a "typical" Novice Mid speaker or listener or reader or writer, but each example must be treated as a unique creation, *produced by the individual on his or her own terms.* Although extremely unlikely given the nature of the proficiency level involved, it is conceivable to find a Novice High speaker who regularly uses the past passive tense of a given Indo-European language, while being unable to use the present active tense in a consistent manner. It is also possible for a speaker to perform at the Advanced Level with a vocabulary of only 1000 words. While there are structural and lexical phenomena which normally stake out the territory of a given performance level, we cannot make these phenomena the sole descriptors of proficiency.

We are all proficient in languages. The language we call our native or first language will probably, depending on the extent of formal background and the variety of experiences, be measured by the ACTFL proficiency guidelines as anywhere from Advanced to Superior, with Superior following the ILR scale from Level 3 to Level 5. I suspect that I am proficient in speaking at the Novice Low Level in any number of languages, including Japanese, Chinese, Spanish, French, German, Russian, and Swedish, and would hope to be rated considerably more proficient in at least one of these. The point is that most of us can be rated in any of the languages in which we have had formal training and even in languages that we may have acquired informally, through travel or family or neighborhood. This fact alone should give us a considerable sense of accomplishment, regardless of the number of quizzes we have passed or the number of courses we have completed. Proficiency-based curricula, materials, evaluation procedures, and research can tell us all something measurable about our performance in whatever language or language skill area we choose. Although its applications are not yet fully understood, proficiency promises to put our teaching and learning on a more realistic basis than at any time in recent memory, without sacrificing the years of methodological, psychological, and psychometric development that the profession has undergone. To quote Asher, one can learn a foreign language by *any* method or technique at all, as long as there is enough time devoted to achieving proficiency (Asher 2, p. 213). In other words, proficiency is the outcome of language learning. It is not a method. It is not a set of materials. It is not a set of classroom techniques. It is not a battery of tests. It is not a psychological model in and of itself. It represents all of these aspects without diminishing the value that each contributes.

Proficiency is fast becoming a movement within the profession. As with most movements, we could be witnessing the construction of another bandwagon, with the usual handbills and hoopla, if "proficiency" takes over where "audiolingualism," "communicative competence," and "individualization of instruction" have gone before. It is not the intention of the profession to allow "proficiency" to become simply another buzzword, leading us to view a complex phenomenon as reduceable to a set of formulaic techniques divorced from the realities of our classrooms, programs, and schools. Proficiency represents the basic principle upon which our profession has operated for centuries, namely, to help others control their personal and social environments by means of language and to obtain the greatest benefit from interaction with those environments, such as the school and street, the classroom and the boardroom, the casual conversation and the prepared speech, wherever it is possible to acquire or learn the skills of the language.

Proficiency in a Changing Profession ─────────────

Change is occurring in the profession at a pace that makes reporting difficult. Previous ACTFL volumes have frequently reported on topics which were already thoroughly researched. This year's volume, by contrast, is marked by many references to personal communications and forthcoming publications. Even as these words are being typed, there is work being done to support one or more of the hypotheses presented in the following chapters. One example involves the teaching of German at Portland State University (Portland, Oregon) in its Department of Foreign Languages. The German section of the department has reoriented its entire first-year program in the direction of proficiency learning and evaluation, even going so far as to set aside a separate room in which oral proficiency testing is conducted on a continuous basis. Students are expected to come to the testing center at least four times each quarter to participate in interviews with an examiner on the kinds of topics already practiced in class, although students are not "prepped" for the exact topics to be discussed. As much as 45 percent of the student's final grade is based on performance on the oral examinations. In addition, the German teaching staff has geared their grading policy to reflect the ACTFL guidelines, translating the level attained on the oral proficiency interviews into traditional letter grades. Thus, by the end of the two-quarter intensive sequence, students receive a C+ for Novice High performance in speaking, with an A awarded for Intermediate High performance. The other 55 percent of the final grade in the courses is determined by performance on written tests and by participation in day-to-day classroom activities. Although details of the program have yet to appear in print (Fischer, 3), it should be noted here that the staff at Portland State University seems to have already realized both the potential and the problems involved in using oral proficiency testing as the "organizing principle" for their particular program. They teach toward the test by practicing the kinds of questions and situations used in the interviews. However, since each interview is different and the student still has to perform, the memorization of pat answers and the exhibition of "hothouse specials" can be easily redirected by appropriate interruptions and cross-checking of student responses during the interview. The results reported to date are encouraging (4).

All of this leaves us with a number of questions still to be answered from the discussion of proficiency as an organizing principle for research, curriculum development, and evaluation.

What should the relationship be between traditional grades and ratings in the ACTFL guidelines?

It may be unwise, and potentially unfair, to base a course grade on any one aspect of a course, no matter how basic that aspect may be viewed by the profession. I personally feel that *all* students completing a one-year university-level "elementary" language course should be able to perform at the Novice High Level or above in speaking. They are normally exposed to the kinds of language needed at the Advanced Plus Level, even if they do not always receive ample opportunity to practice Advanced Plus language to the point of mastery demanded by the proficiency descriptions. In any event, all students in first-year university programs should be able to use the target language at the Novice High Level with no difficulty. However, whether or not performance at Novice High should be made a prerequisite for earning at least a D in a course is a decision best left to the supervisor of the given course sequence. At the same time, the experiences reported by Fischer (3, 4) indicate that if students are encouraged (by practice) and motivated (by grades) to perform at Novice High and above, they will in fact actually attain that level. Magnan, in chapter 4, suggests some of the intervening steps needed to help students integrate what they learn structurally and lexically—that is, on an achievement basis—with how they perform in terms of proficiency.

What is the relationship between speaking and other skill areas?

If students learn to deal with language based on their experiences of the world, chances are very good that they will both understand what they are doing in a language class and will retain the skills that they have learned over a long period of time. This fact demands a variety of materials and sequences, as well as an integration of the various skill areas. After all, we do not experience the world through the written word alone or solely in a classroom setting or only through interaction with a teacher. The speaking skill area, through the Oral Proficiency Interview, has served as the focus of attention for the profession up to now. However, there is evidence that skill in listening should be at least as high on the proficiency scale, if not higher, than speaking. Yet this hypothesis has been put to very few empirical tests. How great should the difference be between listening and speaking? What kinds of materials are most appropriate for stimulating active listening? What, as well, should students be reading and writing in order to stabilize their speaking and listening skills? Has the profession perhaps placed too much emphasis on speaking, in the hope that the other skill areas will more or less fall into line behind it? In Chapter 1, Lowe suggests some of the research needed to answer these questions. And Bragger, in Chapter 3, gives samples of the kinds of materials needed to integrate speaking with other skill areas.

What should the proper sequence be for formal language instruction?

Traditionally, most beginning language courses have been guided by "the grammar syllabus." Materials have been arranged and exercises have been developed in order to practice a particular verb tense or a particular adjectival phrase structure. The actual communicative content of a given set of materials and exercises has all too frequently been accorded secondary importance. A "proficiency syllabus," however, would be radically different in its orientation. Structure serves content rather than the other way around. What is produced orally or in writing is subordinate to what is intended by the speaker or writer. The complete sentence is replaced by situationally appropriate words and phrases. The error is corrected only after the listener or reader has taken in and evaluated the entire utterance. In Chapter 2, Heilenman and Kaplan give specific suggestions for the arrangement of materials and teaching strategies in a proficiency-oriented curriculum. Buck and Forsythe (Chapter 5) outline the kinds of learning strategies at work in the world of business, which has classrooms with highly flexible and pragmatic scheduling and content.

This year's ACTFL volume follows closely upon last year's. Indeed, one title suggested for the volume was "Learning from Proficiency: The Unifying Principle," to underscore the continuity of theme between the two volumes. We are seeing the profession develop a renewed identity around proficiency, which has necessitated the continuation of the topic within the ACTFL series. There is much of a practical nature about proficiency that unites various subdisciplines within our profession and which will unite us more as we gain experience with the phenomenon.

Proficiency on the Outside

In an extremely entertaining book about the culture and language of Japan, Jack Seward, an American businessman with over thirty years of experience living and working in Japan, vents his irritation at those of his countrymen who claim that other Americans of mutual acquaintance are completely "fluent" in Japanese, but who offer no qualification for the claim; it is either "fluent" or nothing at all (7). He expresses his exasperation by indicating that he wishes he had ten yen for every American in Japan who stated that his or her child speaks the language "just like a native"; he would gladly return all those ten-yen coins one hundredfold on the day he met one such child who was even one quarter as good as the advanced publicity proclaimed (p. 195). He proceeds, in a section appropriately entitled "Testing Linguistic Ability," to set forth what can justifiably be called a set of proficiency guidelines for the foreigner in Japan who wants to survive in Japanese, including function, content, and accuracy statements based on activities such as translating a Japanese newspaper article into English, speaking in Japanese on the telephone (as a test of accent), interpreting a taped conversation between two natives, giving the meaning of one hundred technical words and phrases understood by a Japanese college student, reading the first twenty signs sighted on a street in a Japanese city, and giving a ten-minute impromptu talk on an everyday topic. Seward even suggests a rating scale, with gradations from AAA, AA, and A, through B, C, D, E, down to F, FF, and FFF (p. 196). He does not, of course, elaborate on the scale, since he is trying to underscore with humor the serious matter of determining just how well someone speaks modern Japanese. Aside from the satisfaction a person might receive from learning that he or she is better than or not as good as someone else, Seward writes that such a proficiency-based language test "would provide vital data to would-be employers in all fields, many of whom have been painfully stung in the past after hiring foreigners whose actual ability in Japanese turned out to be many notches below their self-stated ability" (p. 196).

The point of mentioning Seward's observations about self-proclaimed vs. actual "fluency" in Japanese is to emphasize that thinking in terms of proficiency is nothing new or radical or incomprehensible to most people, even with relatively little formal exposure to the intricacies of the Oral Proficiency Interview. It is possible for a perceptive businessperson, as it is for the experienced classroom teacher, to determine what we should be observing in proficient speakers, listeners, readers, or writers of a given target language, and to adapt our teaching techniques, as well as their learning strategies, accordingly. There is no mystery to proficiency; it simply reflects what language is and what language does, nothing less.

Heilenman and Kaplan present us with three scenarios for the immediate future of proficiency. Although the discussion is loaded in favor of one of these future visions of the profession, we should not become complacent that one of the other prophecies for the year 1994 won't come true. The language teaching profession in the United States of America is in a position to make itself felt as a significant force in the educational community. Let us discuss everything openly and in a spirit of collegiality, realizing that for the first time in the history of our profession we seem to be able to understand how to accomplish what may have eluded us ever since the first language class was instituted: the ability to help others acquire a set of skills necessary for basic human survival and for constructive individual development.

In closing there is a saying by the German humorist Wilhelm Busch, which he could have borrowed from the Chinese:

Es gibt nichts Gutes,
Außer: man tut es.
There is nothing (which is) good,
Except: you do it.

Postscript _____

Throughout the volume, reference will be made to the guidelines or the proficiency guidelines. These are the *ACTFL Provisional Proficiency Guidelines* (1). In order to establish terminology that we can use meaningfully, without, at the same time, creating unnecessary jargon, the four levels (plus sublevels) in the guidelines will be referred to as Novice Low, Novice Mid, Novice High; Intermediate Low, Intermediate Mid, Intermediate High; Advanced, Advanced Plus; and Superior. The generic descriptions for the various levels are given in Appendix A. Wherever the proficiency scales developed by the Interagency Language Roundtable (ILR) are discussed, the terms used will be: Level 0(+), Level 1(+), Level 2(+), Level 3(+), Level 4(+), and Level 5. The definitions for the ILR levels are given in Appendix B. The history of the ILR and ACTFL proficiency scales is outlined in detail by Liskin-Gasparro (6). As far as possible, the terms *intermediate* and *advanced* will be avoided, so as not to create the impression that a student rated Intermediate Mid in speaking or Advanced in writing is necessarily in a second-year or third-year university course currently labeled "Intermediate Conversational Spanish" or "Advanced French Composition."

References, Learning from Proficiency: The Unifying Principle

1. *ACTFL Provisional Proficiency Guidelines.* Hastings-on-Hudson, NY: American Council on the Teaching of Foreign Languages, 1982.
2. Asher, James, J. "The Total Physical Response," pp. 324–31 in Harris Winitz, ed., *Native Language and Foreign Language Acquisition.* New York: New York Academy of Sciences, 1981, quoted by Simon Belasco, "Time, Proficiency, and the Best Method: An Editorial." *The Modern Language Journal* 67, 3 (1983): 213–15.
3. Fischer, William B. "Not Just Lip Service: Systematic Oral Testing in a First-Year College German Program." Manuscript, 36 pages.
4. _____. Personal communication, 1984.
5. Higgs, Theodore V. "Language Teaching and the Quest for the Holy Grail," pp. 1–9 in Theodore V. Higgs, ed., *Teaching for Proficiency, the Organizing Principle.* The ACTFL Foreign Language Education Series, vol. 15. Lincolnwood, IL: National Textbook Co., 1984.
6. Liskin-Gasparro, Judith E. "The ACTFL Proficiency Guidelines: A Historical Perspective," pp. 11–42 in Theodore V. Higgs, ed., *Teaching for Proficiency, the Organizing Principle.* The ACTFL Foreign Language Education Series, vol. 15. Lincolnwood, IL: National Textbook Co., 1984.
7. Seward, Jack. *Japanese in Action. An Unorthodox Approach to the Spoken Language and the People Who Speak It.* New York: Walker/Weatherhill, 1969.

1

The ILR Proficiency Scale as a Synthesizing Research Principle: The View from the Mountain

Pardee Lowe, Jr.
Interagency Language Roundtable

Introduction

This chapter examines and evaluates current major goals in foreign language teaching and suggests a better way to identify, define, and attain realistic alternatives by using the ILR proficiency scale as a synthesizing research principle. The chapter examines the ILR proficiency system's adaptability across time to show its suitability for this task. Employing the metaphor of climbing a mountain, we propose six hypotheses relating to proficiency-oriented teaching. The first two hypotheses relate to listening comprehension ability exceeding or lagging behind speaking ability for certain students. The next two hypotheses concern the integration of culture as reflected in students' target language speech. The fifth hypothesis suggests achieving accelerated output through a combination of factors apparently diametrically opposed to those proposed by Krashen. The last hypothesis proposes that a threshold readiness level exists below which government immersion programs are not successful. Using these six hypotheses, we discuss the scale's value as a synthesizing research principle for all levels of foreign language teaching.

A general knowledge of the Interagency Language Roundtable (ILR) Proficiency Scale and of the Oral Proficiency Interview (OPI) is assumed.

Pardee Lowe, Jr. (Ph.D., University of California, Berkeley) is former chair of the ILR Testing Committee and currently is Chief of Testing at the Central Intelligence Agency's Language School. He consults widely on language testing. A member of the ACTFL Guidelines Project, he has focused on the guidelines' commensurability with the government scales so that a national standard might evolve. He has trained both government and academic oral proficiency interviewers in over thirty-six languages, wrote the government handbook on oral proficiency testing, and writes regularly on oral and written test design and administration. He is a member of ACTFL, AATG, CALICO, and TESOL.

The designation *ILR* more accurately expresses proficiency's present position in the government foreign language training and testing community. Besides the U.S. Department of State's Foreign Service Institute (FSI), several federal agencies—the Central Intelligence Agency, the Federal Bureau of Investigation, the National Security Agency, and the Peace Corps, among others—also employ this testing procedure.

On the nature of the ILR scale and the OPI in general, see Jones (28, 29), Clark (12), Lowe (39, 43, 44), Wilds (59), and Lowe and Liskin-Gasparro (48). On testing reading and listening, see Byrnes (5), Canale (6), Phillips (51), and the accompanying response papers, Larson and Jones (35, pp. 113–38), and Jones (30).

Goals

Attaining any level of foreign language proficiency is praiseworthy. Too often, however, the profession has castigated itself for failing to achieve its goals, such as instilling a love of the foreign culture, its literature, and its language, as well as trying to teach nativelike proficiency. Rather, we should recognize our courage in undertaking so much.

The ILR proficiency scale, and its academic counterpart, the ACTFL/ETS scale, reveal the full extent of these goals. In the ILR experience, a well-educated native requires roughly twenty-four years of exposure and practice in the language (from mother's knee to graduate diploma) to attain high-level mastery.

Why then do foreign language teachers and researchers bemoan their students' failure to scale such heights in three years at high school or a year and a half at college, or six months at a government language school? In this regard, America's strength, "the quick study," is also her weakness. An Air Force general, so an apocryphal story goes, once inquired about the length of a Chinese speaking course. "Two years, sir," came the answer. "Why hell," he erupted, "that's longer than it takes to train a jet fighter pilot." Two years represents a drop in the bucket to acquire the verbal expression system of one of this planet's oldest and richest cultures!

To counteract America's love affair with "the quick study," the profession must realign foreign language learning with those skills requiring an equally long period of study and development, namely, music and sports. Sports pervade American life. You can see your progress: you sink that putt, leap that hurdle, return that serve. These are all way stations to winning the game. Similarly, the foreign language field must identify realistic interim goals and discover effective ways of attaining these realistic way stations to language mastery.

ILR and ACTFL/ETS oral proficiency workshops have helped articulate realistic goals for the foreign language teaching profession. ACTFL, ETS, and the ILR regularly conduct proficiency testing workshops. Along with short familiarization presentations, ACTFL and ETS have presented five-day workshops, leading to tester certification, and special programs like the ACTFL/Harrison (NY) School District program to investigate possible high school level curriculum changes implied by proficiency, and the ACTFL/NEH three-week workshop at Haverford College, Haverford, Pennsylvania, to acquaint high school teachers with the system and to design proficiency-based high school curricular materials. These workshops have helped identify realistic goals for the foreign language teaching profession. The ability to survive for a day or two in the foreign country (Level 1/Intermediate) constitutes a workable end goal and certainly a respectable interim goal, as does being able to live abroad on the economy (Level 2/Advanced). Finally, both government and academia applaud the attainment of ILR Level 3/Superior at which the user can discuss both abstract and concrete topics, resolve unfamiliar problem situations, hypothesize, and support opinion. In a genuinely proficiency-based French and Spanish course with motivated students, trained teachers, appropriate materials, and careful focus, for example, Level 0+/Novice High probably represents a high, yet attainable goal in a three-year proficiency-based high school course; Level 1+/Intermediate High in a year-and-a-half proficiency-based college course; and Level 2+/Advanced Plus in a six-month proficiency-based government intensive course.

Still, much about the attainment of these goals eludes us. Testing and research avail little if they cannot be rapidly interpreted by the disparate groups of foreign language instructors and researchers in academia, business, and government. The metaphor of scaling the Language Acquisition Mountain illustrates our present situation.

The Language Acquisition Mountain

Attaining the peak—with God, mothers, and high achievers

Three parties set out to climb a mountain, the Language Acquisition Mountain. The members of the first party lacked time for planning. So they seized their ice picks, fastened on their crampons and other gear, and scaled the mountain's sheer face. They lost many climbers. But in the end a few reached the peak. Others achieved various heights along the way. This was an ILR group, which developed a proficiency scale capable of reflecting top performance at the peak, and were themselves Levels 3+, 4, 4+, and a very few 5s.

Reaching the base camp

Members of a second party found an easier way, at least initially. They climbed a less steep path to the tree line, establishing a base camp from which to discover the best route and methods to scale the peak. This group consisted of intermediate climbers, Levels 1+, 2, 2+, and 3/Intermediate, High, Advanced, Superior.

Practicing at the foot

A third party consisted of novice mountain climbers who camped at the foot of the mountain to learn which face to scale and the different techniques required. They were trained by high school and college teachers and by language acquisition researchers at ACTFL/ETS Novice and Intermediate levels.

The metaphor leads to an insight. Three disparate views of language acquisition exist, as do three distinct groups that have acquired language at various levels of proficiency. These provide the view from the foot of the mountain, the view from the base camp, and the view from the peak.

Each view possesses *part* of the truth. How can each view be tested against some larger criterion, measured against a constant scale? How can the views be seen from vantage points other than those of the present language researchers? Can they be linked?

In our opinion, the ILR scale that has served government testing and teaching for thirty years as an "organizing principle" links each view. Would it fulfill the same task for our research? Could it take us even further, synthesizing past studies, integrating present studies, and directing future studies? In short, could proficiency become a synthesizing principle informing the three views? And if unable to reconcile the views, then, to guide research into their differences?

Using the ILR proficiency scale as an organizing principle, this chapter compares the three views, suggesting that proficiency not only organizes testing, classroom methodology, and curriculum design but also affords a golden opportunity to mount research efforts synthesizing all three views, linking the unique insights of the language acquisition researchers, the practical pedagogy of ILR language teachers, and the unique experience of those few successful high-level language learners (Levels 3+ to 5) who neared or scaled the peak.

History

What characteristics does the ILR proficiency scale possess that lend it, in particular, to the task of synthesizing language acquisition research? This chapter suggests that the ILR proficiency scale possesses a unique combination of characteristics. To understand this unique combination, a review of the ILR scale's history and adaptation are in order.

The ILR system arose to fulfill a State Department need, namely, to test the functional foreign language ability of Foreign Service Officers. The term *system* is used in the specific sense of a set of level definitions and a rating procedure that applies to all languages *and* language skill modalities; *system* is not employed in the sense of a monolithic, bureaucratic set of procedures. The following section details the growth in concepts that allow one to speak of an ILR system.

The system encompasses the full range of language performance in the four skill modalities from Novice to Educated Native Speaker. (See Figure 1.) Historically, the ILR has devoted most of its attention to speaking, some attention to reading, and much less to listening and writing. As of 1983 the tasks are commensurate in nature and difficulty at each level across the four skills. As of 1981 a derivative commensurate scale capable of better assessing learner outcomes at the scale's lower end exists from ACTFL/ETS. *Derivative* means that the ILR scale provides the source for the ACTFL/ETS scale; and *commensurate* signifies that scores obtained from interviews rated on the ACTFL/ETS scale agree with the major levels on the ILR scale. (See Liskin-Gasparro, 36.) The *Australian Second Language Proficiency Ratings* scale (ASLPR by Ingram and Wylie, 27) furnishes an example of a derivative, yet incommensurate scale due to the replacement of the ILR's classic Educated Native Speaker (ENS) by more work-related or job-specific language users. The development of the ACTFL/ETS scale indicates the differing foci of academic and government training. Despite the current difference in basic interests, ILR and ACTFL/ETS look forward to the day when they will produce higher-level target language speakers, readers, etc. The congruence of these two scales permits an expanded scale for research work: the ACTFL/ETS scale at the lower end and the ILR scale at the upper end.

This is but one example of the scale's adaptability to new groups of users. Others have devised scales as well. For example, there is Schumann's *basilang, mesolang,* and *acrolang* continuum, which focuses on more accurate classification of low-range (in the ILR sense) language acquisition behaviors. Hinofotis et al. (24) conducted a small study to ascertain how Schumann's scale relates to the ILR scale. Using general (non-ILR-type) interviews, they examined the level of the ILR grammar factor and found the following tentative equivalencies (bearing in mind that the equivalencies refer to a single factor, not to the global rating):

Figure 1. ILR Skills—Capsule Characterization

Level 5

(Educated native) Functions equivalent to a well-educated native. (Special Purpose Mode)

absolutely appropriate discourse in wide range of contexts from colloquial to careful formal speech

---

Level 4

(Representation) Tailors language to suit audience. (Projective Mode)

well-organized discourse (synonyms controlled)

Level 3

(Abstract) Thinks in TL. Supports opinion. Hypothesizes. Handles unfamiliar situations, topics. (Evaluative Mode)

organized discourse (general vocabulary controlled, only sporadic errors in basic grammar, some errors in frequent complex structures, more errors in low-frequency complex structures, colloquial to careful formal speech)

Level 2

(Concrete) Operates in past and future as well as present time. (Instructive Mode)

paragraphs (combining sentences into limited connected discourse)

Level 1

(Survival) Consistently creates with language. Tends to operate in present time. (Orientation Mode)

short sentences

Level 0+

Operates with memorized material. (Enumerative Mode)

short lists (gathering building blocks)

Level 0

No functional ability

(next to) nothing

---

basilang appears to cover the ILR Level 0–1 range; *mesolang,* ILR 1 + –2/ 2 +; and *acrolang,* 2/2 + and up. Such a scale reflects second language acquisition's focus on detailed case or longitudinal studies which might be called *microresearch* (small segments of the mountain, say, the first one hundred feet). In contrast, ILR investigations reflect larger *n*s and larger patterns of strength and weakness: these tend to characterize at least a level, if not whole sets of such patterns describing several levels. ILR work might, therefore, be termed *macroresearch.* Both types are needed and supplement one another.

Why Adaptation Is Necessary—The Dynamic Nature of Proficiency

An individual's language proficiency fluctuates. Moreover, each skill reflects a different dynamic level. Oral proficiency changes constantly; listening proficiency fluctuates depending on use; reading proficiency achieves stasis over longer periods of time; the stability of writing has not been investigated. If research bears out these observations (Lowe, 42), the results will have implications for foreign language teaching. Empirically verifying these trends demands an evaluation procedure sensitive to language's *dynamis* and *stasis,* to its fluctuation and stability. We require a procedure that grows in accuracy as our knowledge about foreign language proficiency increases. Just such growth took place in deriving the ACTFL/ETS scale from the ILR scale in the late 1970s and early 1980s, a move that brings us closer to describing the mountain more fully.

Three aspects of ILR proficiency

The ILR proficiency scale operates according to gestalt psychological theory, implicitly includes many facets of current linguistic theory, and provides a general, rather than a specific, rating of foreign language ability. Each point must be examined.

Proficiency's gestalt nature. The last aspect to be investigated, the gestalt nature of the ILR proficiency scale, so pervades the system that gestalt must be discussed first. In part, the discrete-point testing background prevalent in the 1950s, 1960s, and early 1970s also makes the following statement necessary: *the ILR system is not a discrete-point system.*

The ILR system operates by assigning a global score, not by adding part scores to obtain a total. A mountain climber does not analyze the rock and soil to determine his location; instead he looks at the overall shape of the mountain. Similarly, testers do not scrutinize individual vocabulary items or grammatical structures but assess how a candidate integrates them into the total performance (the OPI, for example, is an integrative test). Testers measure a candidate's performance against the area delimited—but not exhaustively described—by the ILR proficiency definitions. Having identified a performance clearly indicative of a specific level, testers assign that level.

This procedure corresponds to any approach where an outstanding performance constitutes a reference point and subsequent performances are compared with the classic (standard) performance: high diving and figure skating are two nonlinguistic examples.

Such a performance or figure is a *gestalt*. A gestalt reflects a psychological entity whose whole exceeds or at least differs from the sum of its parts. The trained oral interview rater instantly recognizes those performances which come closest to matching the classic sample of a given level. The gestalt nature of the ILR system has extensive ramifications for ILR rating and elicitation. (For more on gestalt theory and the dynamics of rating, etc., see Lowe, 45.)

Proficiency and implicitness. Since ILR definitions outline the essential gestalt but do not exhaustively describe each level, means that much in the use of the system remains implicit. This affects the work described below. For this reason, training in the ILR testing procedures is required. For this reason, too, some who received oral interview training prior to 1980 might claim that the system has changed, while those working consistently in the system tend to see these so-called changes not as new but rather as objectification of aspects present from the system's inception. For example, before 1979 one rarely discussed "discourse organization" within the ILR system. Yet no experienced rater, past or present, would assign a high-level rating to an "incoherent/incohesive" sample. The system's higher levels imply control of discourse.

Proficiency, performance, achievement. Finally, before examining the scale's adaptability to new theories, we define both the nature and extent of proficiency and the kinds of performances to which the designation *proficiency* truly applies. This demarcation stresses the narrowest possible view. Elsewhere we define the nature of ILR proficiency (Lowe, 45) by stating that *proficiency equals achievement (functions,* content, accuracy) plus functional evidence of internalized strategies for creativity,* i.e., to be proficient you must be able to use the language. Here, we stress the extent to which proficiency must be reflected in performance: *proficiency is the*

---

*The term *functions* is employed here to mean fixed *task universals* that characterize specific levels in the ILR system. It is not used in the functional/notional sense of a set of variable qualifiers affecting language communication (Munby, 49). If the domain tested is too narrow or if the concept of proficiency is too limited or if proficiency is equated with achievement above the ACTFL/ETS Novice Low and Mid levels, then definitional and rating chaos ensues.

global rating of general language ability over a wide range of functions and topics at any given level.

We purposely avoid a global statement of ability in a limited area, such as a rating based on the ability to pronounce French acceptably for a musical performance of four songs by Debussy. Both the domain, four songs, and the task, pronunciation, are too limited to count as proficiency. We likewise avoid certifying an oral interview proficiency score when the interviewers use a single question type, e.g., descriptive prelude, and the candidate carries out only a single task universal, e.g., narration in the past for five minutes. Many testing experts regard the ILR proficiency rating system as a "performance test." Performance tests contrast with knowledge tests and "require the candidate to demonstrate the skills directly under conditions similar to an actual job situation" (Jones, 32, p. 50). However, while the ILR system does test performance in a technical sense, this view should not be perpetuated in a practical one: the risk of mixing the concepts of proficiency and achievement is too great. *As the system becomes more widely known, this confusion must be avoided at all costs.*

In most cases, the government solution requires language-general tests to provide a score on a candidate's linguistic skill. Cost effectiveness in test design and production is not the only rationale for language-general tests; several government agencies require "transferability." Can one climb as proficiently on snow and ice as on hard rock? This characteristic represents the ability to take one's language proficiency and apply it to another subject area without formal retooling; that is, to know that an employee's linguistic ability does not depend on a specific context or job. *Context-independence* refers here not to the skill existing in a vacuum but rather to the fact that the candidate's grammar, vocabulary, and sociolinguistic/cultural skills (at Level 3) suffice to understand a text without semantic feedback. A chemist thoroughly knowledgeable in his or her specialty may well be able to read an article on a chemical process written in a foreign language. But in cases of doubtful interpretation, he or she resolves the doubt from knowledge of the field, not from a knowledge of the target language. We speak here of the reverse case, that is, where knowledge of the target language suffices to clarify possible misunderstandings. The ability to transfer skills distinguishes Level 3/Superior and above, explaining the government's interest in Level 3 as an exit goal for language training or an entrance goal for new employees.

The problem of transferability occurs in government, too. We notice, for example, that the kinds of tasks and content tested may, for different government employees, fall at opposite ends of the *language-general/job-specific* task continuum. In its strictest sense, a performance test is job specific. A performance test is made up of both test tasks and test conditions closely approximating those on the job (sometimes referred to as a "work sample"). Buck (4) reminds us that job-specific samples without transferability of creativity, lexis, and accuracy to a wider area constitute, by definition, a subset and hence represent achievement, not proficiency. In fact, such a subset likely represents a "hothouse special," that is, a topic memorized or practiced to perfection, which blooms like a rare flower in all its linguistic glory above the rocky and less fertile soil of the candidate's true sustained creativity. Depending on a sample's position on the work-related segment of the continuum, a work-related sample may also represent a subset. (For a government oral test more indicative of the job-specific end of the work-related continuum, see the DLI Recorded Oral English Evaluation designed to test foreign pilot trainees' English at the DLI English Language Center, Lackland, Texas.) Anyone involved in needs analyses requiring the establishment of discrete job categories can envision the multiplicity of tests required to meet such job-specific testing. Energy, time, and financial resources normally do not suffice to create a large number of tests. To guarantee that a test containing such a subset fully qualifies for an ILR proficiency rating, the sample must be expanded and supplemented by speech production on non-job-specific, non-interest areas to assure sustained creativity across a large number of subject areas, that is, to obtain an adequate, ratable sample for a language-general test. We ask not if the candidate can climb a few hundred feet; we ask if he or she can climb significant portions of the mountain.

The language-general test lies at the other end of the continuum. It relates not to testing a specific job but to *testing the linguistic skills generally required to function adequately in the target language.* These skills, in turn, are assumed to be a sine qua non for performing most jobs using the target language. In between stretches a broad category designated *work-related.* The tasks and content of these categories become progressively more work-related as one moves away from the language-general toward the job-specific pole.

The rest of this chapter focuses on the structure of proficiency and the nature of the ILR proficiency scale. A companion piece should one day discuss the nature of ILR testing instruments and procedures: writing tests, listening comprehension and reading comprehension tests, the oral interview, and the reading interview. In a reading interview, the candidate summarizes in English target language passages graded according to the ILR reading proficiency scale. Due to its historical importance, the oral interview will be referred to, but no attempt is made to treat it exhaustively. Instruments for the other skills are mentioned only in passing.

Reflecting Theory: A Retrospective

How does one describe a mountain? How does one gauge the adequacy of the description? Can the approach adopted describe foothills, titans, and volcanoes? How does the description of mountains reflect such theories as tectonics? Foreign language research seeks an approach that describes the Language Acquisition Mountain as we see it today but that is flexible enough to deal with new insights tomorrow.

The ILR system's adaptability has been amply demonstrated. New theories across time have often been shown to be implicit in the system and their insights assimilated to expand our consciousness of how the scale functions, of what to elicit in obtaining a ratable sample, and of how to assign ratings. Each new theory brings a fuller understanding of the structure of proficiency in general and of the nature of the ILR proficiency scale in particular. We highlight the major theoretical developments illuminating the nature of proficiency of the ILR proficiency system, and the principal investigators roughly in chronological order.

The ILR definitions were influenced by the linguistic zeitgeist of the 1950s. The system's theoretical base developed linguistically from Bloomfieldian structuralism and psychometrically from criterion-referenced testing, before it became customary in foreign language evaluation. The scaling technique, based on Osgood's "semantic differential," allows a rater to state the relative amount present of one of a pair of bipolar terms. The terms are placed at either end of a continuum. The rater marks a point along the continuum representing the relative amount. For example, one could state the relative *foreignness* or *nativeness* of a candidate's pronunciation. In the example, the candidate possessed neither a native accent nor a totally American one. Rather, the marking shows a somewhat American accent. (See Figure 2.)

Figure 2. Bipolar Rating Continuum

Pronunciation

Foreign   Native

Later, the polar definitions were supplemented by verbal descriptions of intervening points creating a Likert scale. The descriptions of the contributing factors (accent, fluency, comprehension, vocabulary, and grammar) were written to discourage a one-to-one identification with each of the five levels. Examining factors is akin to a geologist examining types of rock found on a mountain. Such an analysis contributes indirectly to our understanding of what the mountain is like, but it does not directly determine the mountain's height or steepness.

Rice (52) first discussed these factors and their relative weightings. He pointed out that the different factors contributed differently at different levels (his word: "(the factors are) 'unstable' ") and warned against attempting to use one regression equation to capture the factors' contributions. As an experiment a table was devised (based on factor contributions at the Level 2+/3 border) which converted the semantic differential into a Likert scale, allowing raters to add up the factor scores to obtain the global score. Unfortunately, Rice's admonition went unheeded, and the table with its additive scores often replaced proper training in assigning global scores. Clifford (14) demonstrated the insufficiency of such a table, even in modified form with a prediction equation for each base level and plus level (for a total of eleven equations). Global scores so calculated misassigned ratings, at least when compared with those given by experienced raters, almost one third of the time, a percentage of inaccuracy too high for determining government promotions, incentive pay, or overseas duty.

Clifford demonstrated that precisely in those problem cases where new raters needed the table's predictive power, the table rated leniently compared with the ratings assigned by experienced raters. This discrepancy, he believes, results from the noncompensatory nature of the scale and from the varying factor weightings. (See Figures 3 and 4.) Human raters, trained in the system, cope with these variations more effectively than any table.

Several additional experiences called into question both the nature of the factors' contribution and number. Chief among them was the application for the proficiency system to a new clientele, the Peace Corps. Peace Corps volunteers often communicated on concrete topics with remarkable ease *and* inaccuracy. The "Peace Corps syndrome" became a phrase for referring to this combination, subsequently identified as part of a performance continuum from "school" through "classic" to "street" and, in its most extreme form, "terminal" by Lowe (40), and elaborated on by Clifford (15), and by Higgs and Clifford (23).

Hence, the traditional five Foreign Service Institute factors were revamped. Two solutions are current. At the Foreign Service Institute, the traditional five factors [accent (pronunciation), fluency, comprehension, vocabulary, and grammar] were in part renamed, in part recombined, and in part redefined (Adams and Argoff, 1). These changes owe much to Argoff's conceptualizations.

Comprehension was retained (emphasizing the oral interview's earlier interactive nature). Vocabulary was renamed *lexicalization* and expanded to include all the semantic aspects of language. Grammar was combined with accent, since both affect *structural accuracy* (grammar's new designation). And a further factor was added, *discourse competence,* to reflect insights from that field of linguistic endeavor, particularly the nonnative speaker's ability to manage and direct an exchange of information with a target language native. Thus, the Foreign Service Institute's new factors also total five.

Earlier both Lowe (46) and Clifford (16) had questioned the traditional set of five Foreign Service Institute factors and the way in which they had been regarded as contributing to the global score. Lowe referred to them

Figure 3. Inverted Pyramid of Language Proficiency

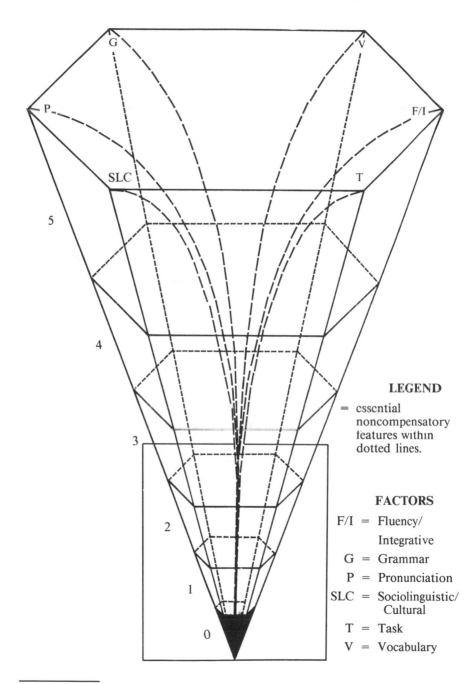

LEGEND

= essential
noncompensatory
features within
dotted lines.

FACTORS

F/I = Fluency/
Integrative

G = Grammar

P = Pronunciation

SLC = Sociolinguistic/
Cultural

T = Task

V = Vocabulary

*Adapted from Clifford, 15.

Figure 4. The ACTFL/ETS Scale and the Inverted Pyramid

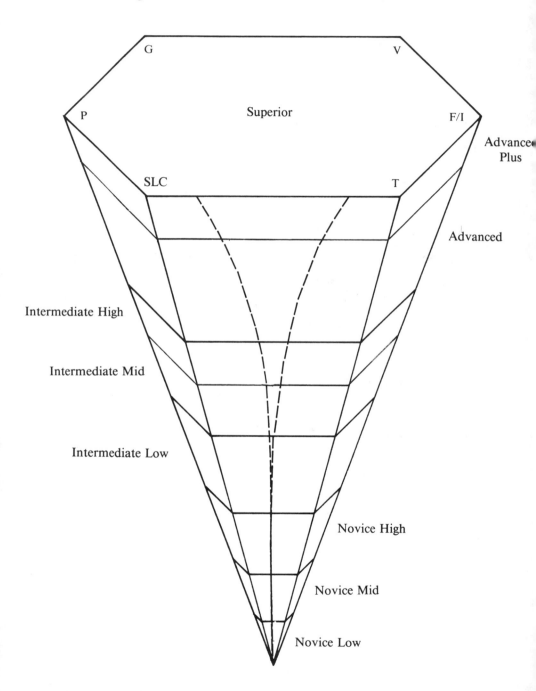

Figure 5. The Dynamic Model

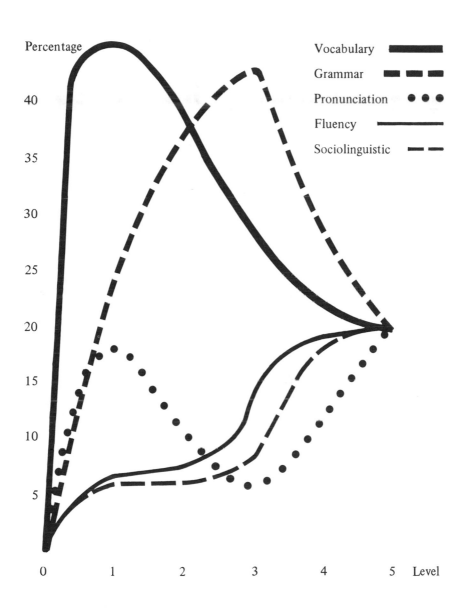

*Reprinted with permission from Higgs and Clifford, "The Push Toward Communication," p. 69 in Theodore V. Higgs, ed., *Curriculum, Competence, and the Foreign Language Teacher.* Lincolnwood, IL: National Textbook Co., 1982.

Figure 6. Speaking Performance Profile

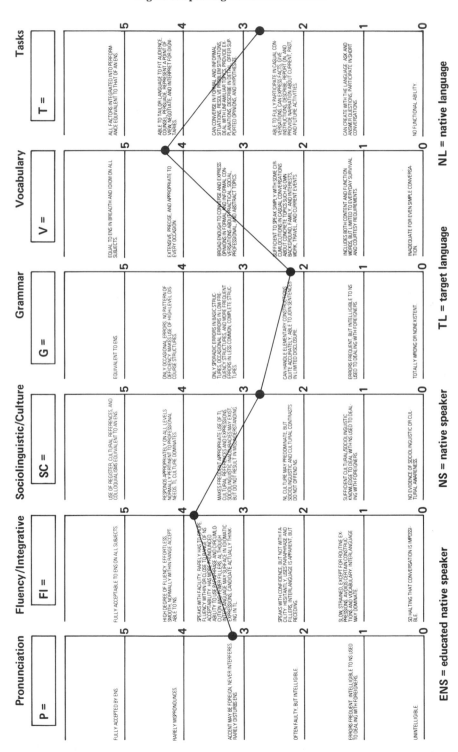

as the *static model* since the now abandoned weighting table statically applied the weightings of the Level 2+/3 border to all levels throughout the scale. Clifford proposed a *dynamic model* which would recognize the uniquely noncompensatory nature of the ILR scale's upper end (Level 3 and higher) and the gradually more compensatory nature of Level 2+ downwards. He also pointed out that even at the lower end, a noncompensatory core exists. (See Figure 5.) The *noncompensatory core* means that despite the fact that Levels 0+ through 2+ often permit compensation, strong vocabulary may offset weaker grammar, some features remain essential and may not be compensated for. Lowe (44) discussed the specifics of noncompensatory material in the more common European languages, namely the necessity for accurate past tense forms, but not complete usage such as the imperfect (*imparfait*) vs. perfect (*preterite/passé composé*) distinction in the Romance and Slavic languages needed to cross the 1+/2 border. A complicating factor in discussing the scale is its exponential growth, which Vincent (57) established through a study in psychophysical scaling with Language School raters and which Clifford depicts graphically in his Inverted Pyramid (Figure 3).

An interagency solution to the factor problem removed comprehension as a factor, since some agencies require a separate listening comprehension score. Both Lowe (46) and Clifford (16) recognized understanding as a separate skill modality and deleted it from among the speaking factors. Vocabulary and grammar were expanded to include insights derived from transformational grammar, discourse analysis, etc. Fluency was redefined from mere ease of speech to the specific requirement for speech rate to fall within the range of rates used by native speakers. As a result of discussions of communicative competence (Hymes, 26), an integrative factor first suggested by Carroll (9) was initially proposed as a separate factor and later combined with fluency. To these four factors yet another was added, the sociolinguistic/cultural factor, occasioned by the necessity for integrating "small c" culture earlier for languages culturally more distant from English, such as Chinese, Japanese, Thai, and Vietnamese. As a result, five profile factors (see Figure 6) emerged, with comprehension a separate ILR score.

In what order do experienced interviewers become conscious of these factors during an interview? Experienced raters reported (Lowe, 44) perceiving pronunciation first; fluency/integrative second; vocabulary third; and the other factors in random order: grammar, sociolinguistic/culture. How comprehensive are these factors? This question can be answered two ways. First with another question: Have all the relevant factors been extracted? It appears that the major ones have been identified. Second, we know that the factors, with slight modification, transfer to the other skill modalities: reading, for example, requires grammar, vocabulary, sociolinguistic/culture with fluency/integrative reflecting reading speed, and pronunciation replaced by its written counterpart, orthography.

Several earlier developments with factors directly led to the present chapter and the search for empirical data to quantify what was otherwise recognized experientially. Clifford (15) applied two concepts—the semantic differential and the Likert scale—by combining earlier Foreign Service Institute factor subscale descriptions with available Language School documents to produce the "Performance Profile," a sheet displaying graphically the five profile factors with verbal descriptions. Marked after the global score has been assigned, the sheet furnishes the candidate, government supervisors, managers, and commanders with a macrodiagnostic statement of the candidate's abilities in each factor area. *Macrodiagnostics* provides a statement of the candidate's performance by factor and reflects how well the candidate uses the language without citing language-specific examples. A macrodiagnostic statement of mountain climbing might report that a climber's footwork is adequate, rope handling ability, superior; coordination, above average; etc. The global rating would state the climber's overall ability to integrate all his or her skills in climbing mountains.

Microdiagnostics contrasts with macrodiagnostics. While the latter makes general statements about factors contributing to overall proficiency, the former provides language-specific detail. For example, a microdiagnostic report would state that at Level 1 the candidate employs some past tense verb forms—often incorrectly formed and used in the wrong contexts (preterite for imperfect, etc.). Lowe (38) dealt with microdiagnostics in a cooperative effort with Language School instructors. Together they developed the so-called "Grammar Grids": lists arranged by proficiency by level of sample grammatical features whose absence, semimastery, or mastery tended to contribute to the global rating. Grids exist in selected languages such as French, German, Italian, Spanish, and Swedish. Grids furnish *confirmatory* but not primary support for the global rating. In all interviews, the extent of successful communication when compared to what an Educated Native Speaker (ENS) would do in the same situation(s) determines the global rating. Grammar Grids reinforce both the concept of "patterns of strengths" and "patterns of errors" in an overall gestalt sense *and* the "one strength/one error rule," which states that a single strength or error counts for nothing. A strength or error must fit a pattern to be significant. One major slip during a climb proves inconsequential. Constant slipping on normally climbable surfaces might be cause for regarding that climber's proficiency as below standard.

Developments in the field of linguistics itself, particularly models of discourse competence, also compelled a reexamination of the factors, their number, their nature, and their contribution. This intense concern with factors ultimately reflects the field's attempt at defining the theoretical model underlying language proficiency. Canale and Swain (7) reviewed various possibilities and suggested a quadripartite division into linguistic, discourse, strategic, and pragmatic competence. This division in turn influenced Bachmann and Palmer (3) in their design for a multi-trait/

multi-method statistical investigation of the interview's construct validity. Their study presented evidence for the oral interview, but not for the reading interview, as a separate method. The Foreign Service Institute's new factors most directly reflect these views, in one case even to the name *discourse competence*. Performance profile factors also take into account these two studies' insights. Answers to the questions of how to slice and label the proficiency pie and its pieces and how the slices contribute to the whole, led to a deeper appreciation of language's complexity and the ILR system's comprehensiveness. (For a highly theoretical discussion of "The Structure of Language Proficiency" in relation to language testing as a whole, see Stevenson, 55 and Vollmer, 58, and the accompanying response papers in Hughes and Porter, 25.)

Between the late 1960s and early 1970s, transformational grammar with its powerful concept of creativity/generativity became part and parcel of ILR ways of discussing the proficiency scale. This influence lives on, chiefly in the characterization of Level 1 (and above) as level(s) of "consistent/sustained creativity" compared with operating predominantly with memorized material at Level 0+.

Clifford and Lowe (18; see also Higgs and Clifford, 23) systematized the ILR definitions statements into three categories: (1) function (task universals), (2) context/content, and (3) accuracy. This Trisection of Oral Proficiency details these categories at each base level (the plus levels are not included). (See Figure 7.) Applying many of the same principles, Clifford, Herzog, and Lowe (19) proposed a Quintasection for Reading (which treats base and plus levels), showing that receptive skills demand a different treatment from productive ones. In contrast to the Oral Trisection's three categories, the Reading Quintasection employs five: (1) reader function, (2) reader accuracy, (3) text type, (4) author accuracy, and (5) author function. The last two affect a passage's overall level. If author accuracy falters or if the author intends a meaning for the piece beyond its apparent surface meaning, then the text's level is raised. For example, Shakespeare's "I come to bury Caesar not to praise him" superficially ranks reading 2+; but to sense its irony demands a higher-level reader. The Trisection and Quintasection supplement the ILR definitions' configurational treatment of these categories by clarifying the general requirements for and interrelationships between each category by level. (On recent reading research and proficiency, see Phillips, 51.)

The performance profile factors' relation to the Oral Trisection's categories presents an interesting problem, particularly with regard to an "anything goes" version of communicative competence. Lowe (44) ascertained that factors relate *dyadically*, not triadically, with each category. Moreover, these relationships are not of equal weight: for each performance profile factor a direct and indirect relationship exists. The pronunciation and the fluency/integrative factors directly relate to function; the sociolinguistic/cultural and vocabulary factors directly relate to context/

Figure 7. Functional Trisection of Oral Proficiency Levels

Level	Functions	Content	Accuracy
ILR Speaking Level			
5	Functions equivalent to an Educated Native Speaker (ENS).	All subjects.	Performance equivalent to Educated Native Speaker.
4	Able to tailor language to fit audience, counsel, persuade, negotiate, represent a point of view, and interpret for dignitaries.	All topics normally pertinent to professional needs.	Nearly equivalent to ENS. Speech is extensive, precise, appropriate to every occasion with only occasional errors.
3	Can converse in formal and informal situations, resolve problem situations, deal with unfamiliar topics, provide explanations, describe in detail, support opinions, and hypothesize.	Practical, social, professional, and abstract topics, particular interests, and special fields of competence.	Errors virtually never interfere with understanding and rarely disturb the ENS. Only sporadic errors in basic structures.
2	Able to fully participate in casual conversations; can express facts; give instructions; describe, report on, and provide narration about current, past, and future activities.	Concrete topics such as own background, family, and interests, work, travel, and current events.	Understandable to NS *not* used to dealing with foreigners; sometimes miscommunicates.
1	Can create with the language; ask and answer questions, participate in short conversations.	Everyday survival topics and courtesy requirements.	Intelligible to an NS used to dealing with foreigners.
0	No functional ability.	None.	Unintelligible.

Task accomplished, attitudes expressed, tone conveyed.

Topics, subject areas, activities, and jobs addressed.

Acceptability, quality, and accuracy of message conveyed.

content; while grammar predictably relates directly to accuracy. Perhaps the most striking finding reveals that *all other factors* (pronunciation, fluency/integrative, sociolinguistic/cultural, and vocabulary) *ultimately affect accuracy,* no matter how indirect the relationship may appear initially. Put another way: *lack or misuse of any factor blocks or distorts communication* (in talking to a target language native unaccustomed to dealing with foreigners). These interrelationships explain two developments in the system: first, how the level definitions could be a configuration; and second, why accuracy is crucial. Accuracy may be a luxury at Level 0+, but by Level 3 it proves indispensable. As an ILR manager so cogently put it: "When you don't understand the target language verb form, it is unsuitable to send a cable back to the States, saying:

'The tanks _____ at the border.'
  a. were   e. should be
  b. are   f. could be
  c. will be   g. had been
  d. might be   h. will have been"

In the early 1980s, the Foreign Service Institute modified its oral testing from a language-general to a more work-related procedure. The new Foreign Service Institute oral interview format begins with a general interview and proceeds through a debriefing to a briefing exercise. In designing this new approach and ways to rate the resulting sample, the Foreign Service Institute introduced insights from transformational grammar and anthropological linguistics, as well as discourse and error analysis. An important aspect of this contribution defines the *nature of oral interview errors* and factors various kinds of errors (intrusive, blocking, etc.) into the rating scale (Adams and Argoff, 1).

Child (10) relates *process* to *product.* He discusses the nature of "texts," by which he means any connected discourse either produced, as in speaking or writing, or understood, as in reading and listening. He draws attention to ILR's emphasis up to now on the extent and nature of a producer/receiver's performance. In contrast, he points to the nature of the product and how it compares with ideal texts produced by natives without nonnative errors. His work influenced ILR reading proficiency and is reflected, for example, in the text type section of the Reading Quintasection. He continues his systematization of differences between ideal native and real nonnative texts by dividing the domain into *codification, textualization,* and *communication* and then describes the subsequent gap between native and nonnative achievement in such texts (11).

Consideration of performance *and* product in relation to the ILR scale and definitions provides yet another vantage point for surveying the system and linking it to academic research with the latter's interest in pragmatics, text linguistics, discourse analysis, etc. Besides American influences (Chomsky, Fillmore), Child's work is strongly influenced by the Danish theoretician, Louis Hjelmselv.

Lowe (39) systematized the OPI's structure, dividing the interview into four phrases horizontally: (1) warm-up, (2) level check, (3) probes, and (4) wind-down; *and* three planes vertically: (1) the psychological, (2) the linguistic, and (3) the evaluative (44). (See Figure 8.) By renaming the linguistic, the substantive plane, one could use the interview to test other than linguistic performance. Canale (6) suggests that such a framework has utility beyond oral tests by applying it to a computer-adaptive test of reading proficiency.

Concerned with the Oral Proficiency Interview's content validity, Lowe (39, 41) also systematized the OPI's elicitation techniques by enumerating and exemplifying question types (the OPI's universal joint) and relating them to ILR levels. He demonstrated that question types do not have a one-for-one correspondence to a level but may serve for one or more levels with varying degrees of efficiency and success. Jones (30) suggested supplementary tasks for strengthening upper level (4–5) OPI content validity (retelling, identifying vocabulary through pictures, etc.). Shohamy (54) demonstrated that the type and extent of the task can affect the global rating.

Lowe (44) suggests that a major difference between neophyte and experienced raters lies less in the ability of both groups to compare a performance with the ILR definitions than in the latter's ability to employ *double triangulation,* to place a candidate's performance between a native speaker's version at the same level and a successful nonnative speaker's version at the same level, while keeping in mind the definition's unique configuration of factors at that level (gestalt). Unfortunately, double triangulation as a technique comes only with extensive experience in rating. He also discussed the gestalt characteristics of the ILR definition at each level and of the *threshold** (rather than midpoint) nature of the ILR rating system, concepts that undergird and pervade the ILR scale, definitions, and rating procedure and profoundly affect applications of the scale. Testers' failure to fully grasp and apply correctly these concepts often leads to misrating in problem cases.

Finally, the ILR definitions themselves, being reflections of "classic" performances or gestalts at each level, were revised in speaking and

---

*The distinction between threshold and midpoint derives from former Chief of the DLIFLC Civilian Personnel Office, Charles Middaugh. *Threshold* refers here to a perceptual gestalt, to a "figure," or to a constellation of factors clearly present to perform the functions in question. In ILR terms, thresholds exist at each plus level/higher base level border: 0+/1, 1+/2, 2+/3, 3+/4, 4+/5. *Threshold* is not used here in the sense of *un niveau-seuil* (Coste, 20), i.e., the minimum amount of language needed to result in communication, most likely reflecting the ILR 0+/1, ACTFL/ETS Novice High/Intermediate Low border.

Figure 8. General Structure of the Oral Proficiency Interview

Four Phases:	Warm-Up	Level Check	Probes	Wind-Down
Three Planes:		(Iterative process)		
Psychological: Verbal reflections	Puts candidate at ease.	Proves to candidate what he or she can do.	Proves to candidate what he or she cannot do.	Returns candidate to level at which he or she functions most accurately.
				Gives candidate feeling of accomplishment.
Linguistic: LS Handbook on question types FSI language-specific questions	Reacquaints candidate with language if necessary.	Checks for functions and content which candidate performs with greatest accuracy.	Checks for functions and content which candidate performs with least accuracy.	(Chance to check that the iterative process is complete.)
Evaluative: Verbal reflections	Gives testers preliminary indication of level of speech and understanding skills.	Finds candidate's S-Level. Finds candidate's U-Level.	Finds level at which candidate can no longer speak accurately. Finds level at which candidate can no longer understand accurately.	(Gives global rating.)

reading by the ILR Testing Committee to reflect the many developments outlined above. The revised definitions make tasks equivalent across skill modalities and introduce verbal descriptions for the ILR plus levels (Lowe, 45). The listening definitions with their mixture of *participative* and *nonparticipative* tasks still require the ILR's attention. Perhaps two sets of definitions are needed.

This section points out that the ILR scale and rating system possesses a wide range of adaptability, but that limits exist since adaptability extends only so far. Discrete-point testing and global proficiency testing clash, and issues arise which should not be treated within a proficiency system.

The ILR proficiency scale provides a tool for gauging the nature and perhaps, to some extent, the success of our research efforts. What happens when the tool is applied to work at the three places on the mountain: the foot, the base camp, and the peak? In general, what does the view from each vantage point look like? How do the views differ? How would proficiency synthesize them?

The Mountain and Research

The ILR scale has existed for only thirty years. The ACTFL/ETS scale has existed for three. The latter scale provides a series of lower-end subranges which should prove valuable in the research suggested here. Consequently, the ACTFL/ETS scale and the ILR scale, which is more sensitive at the higher end, might be profitably combined for research work *in academia, business, and the government.* A further comment from Clark (13) is important: testing following this combined scale is not meant to replace other kinds of testing. Rather, ILR/ACTFL/ETS scale testing can serve as a matrix, a *macroevaluation,* into which diagnostic testing, *microevaluation,* of various areas of interest can and should be fitted. For example, if interested in the Level 2+/Advanced Plus speaker (Higgs and Clifford, 23; Lowe, 44), we could administer Oral Proficiency Interviews to all possible candidates we believe to fall in that range. Then, a diagnostic instrument could also be administered, an instrument designed to ascertain the extent of control in selected grammatical structures whose *mastery* marks the Level 3 speaker but whose *semimastery* characterizes the Level 2+ speaker. The results of the diagnostic instrument could be correlated with a transcript of each oral interview, marked for the grammatical areas of investigation, and with each interview's global score.

The view from the top of the mountain

The view from the peak is awesome, with the distant surrounding terrain and with the path which ascends only so far before forcing climbers to find their own way without maps or guides. No wonder successful climbers rejoice in the accomplishment. For when those at the base camp or at the foot of the mountain talk about how difficult the climb is, those at or near the peak furnish living counterexamples. Levels 5, 4+, 4, and 3+ are indeed achievable. But those at the top stress the paucity of shortcuts, the arduousness of the climb, and the commitment of the climbers. Despite these rigors, they maintain to the last breath that the climb repays the effort.

The view from the foot of the mountain

From the foot of the mountain, the peak is murky; it looms far above, often veiled in mists and buffeted by high winds. The peak seems un-achievable, the sheer face unscalable. But perhaps one can gain courage and skill through practice on the lower slopes. Many individual tech-niques are required to become proficient. The concerns at the foot and at the peak differ. The methods for climbing each vary. The two groups speak in different ways, about different approaches, of paths that seem to lead to different goals. Why the different terminology? How can they talk the same language? Pool their insights? Connect the trails?

Life at the base camp

Unlike the camp at the foot of the mountain that is overflowing with data and theory, research life at the base camp contains less theory than data. The data are more experiential than empirical. Government linguists rarely have the leisure to gather empirical facts, organize them, interpret them, write them up. It is a frustration balanced by the variety of levels encountered with the wealth of data to be researched.

Drawing on ten years of experience with Levels 0–5 in several dozen languages, we advance six hypotheses about base-camp language proficiency and the manner of its acquisition. By and large, the support is experiential, but empirical data will be presented where available. Although empirical data may be preferable, experience that has produced consistent results over thirty years also deserves consideration. Government experience (reported by Higgs and Clifford, 23) formulated the "school," "street," and "terminal" learner distinctions. Their existence is proved by ILR proficiency testing. No study has demonstrated decisively why "street" and "terminal" learners occur. But Clifford (17) suggests that positive reinforcement over time and without correction almost guarantees inaccurate and nonnativelike communication. This represents but one insight gained through government experience.

The base camp's view of the mountain leads to questions and comments about certain hypotheses posed by those working at the foot of the mountain and to new hypotheses posed from the vantage point of the base camp. On the surface, these views appear radically different, even antithetical. But viewed on the ILR proficiency scale, they might prove complementary. But until we attempt synthesis, we will never know.

Synthesis at work: the affective filter and the OPI

The affective filter hypothesis is a case in point. Language acquisition researchers stress the need for teachers to attend constantly to the affective filter. Yet, government instructors note that while at the foot of the mountain it appears mandatory, at the base camp or peak it rarely interferes. ILR experience suggests that at ILR mid and upper ranges the filter stays down almost automatically. Where then is the evidence?

The Oral Proficiency Interview possesses a striking analog to the affective filter, the OPI's psychological plane. In ILR testing experience, interviewers induce the candidate to talk at Levels 0–1 by attending consistently to the psychological plane. At these levels it is often the testers' major preoccupation. But in mid-level tests—except for the relatively short mid-level warm-ups, wind-downs, and probes—the psychological plane receives little attention. Moreover, high-level tests, unless a personally offensive topic is broached, rarely take into account the psychological plane.

Other reasons suggest that the affective filter need not be a mid-level or higher-level problem. Chief among them is government employees' instrumental, if not integrative, motivation, not to mention their preselection at some schools for language-learning aptitude. The effects of these points bear investigation.

The implication remains that pedagogy exists that successfully lowers the filter and maintains it in that position, allowing teachers to devote their attention to other matters. We have yet to determine exactly what these techniques are and what components contribute to their effectiveness. These questions should be researched. A possible approach would place a linguist from academia and a linguist from the government in a government language class to observe and then compare notes from their various vantage points. Perhaps this collaborative observation would identify the unique component(s) that contribute to ILR success in the mid ranges (Levels 1+ through 3) and could also lead to increased efficiency.

This example of the affective filter and the Oral Proficiency Interview suggests how the ILR proficiency scale and the accompanying government testing and teaching experiences can synthesize: by providing a common metric for measuring results, by pooling experiences, by specifically noting the similarities and differences, by providing a framework that will integrate future studies both into the nature of foreign language proficiency and into its acquisition in all four skills.

This chapter does not present a thorough review and synthesis of current acquisition theories and methods—a task admirably executed by Long (37). Our goal here is to suggest that synthesis is desirable, possible, achievable, and rewarding. To achieve synthesis, however, parties in all three camps—at the foot, base, and peak—must explicitly state and test the hypotheses their vantage point suggests are most plausible. We turn now to six such hypotheses—six base-camp hypotheses—to the data and experiences underlying them, and to their implications for language acquisition research. It lies in the nature of hypotheses that ultimately they will be debated, tested, and revised. In that spirit, we propose the following.

Six Base-Camp Hypotheses

We begin with two hypotheses for which data exist and then present other hypotheses owing their existence to the experiences of ILR instructors and testers rather than to thorough investigation.

To understand why data neither suffice nor exist for most of the other hypotheses, we examine the nature of government foreign language data bases. Most information needed to carry out such studies barely exists, is scattered, or is hard to retrieve. Unfortunately, for the most burning question—government time-to-proficiency—data are not generally available either within or across individual agencies. Existing data are often incomplete, inconsistent, and not formatted either to answer the questions posed here or to permit easy access to the answers (Lowe, 42). Data bases are gradually being built, so help is on the way. Other variables, such as aptitude and motivation, play a role. Yet they are not always assessed, again rendering the data hard to work with. Surprisingly, these lacunae exist despite the government's overriding concern for how long it takes to produce a Level 3. On the one hand, we lament this lack of data. On the other, the situation provides us an opportunity to design studies commensurate with a wider view, to link the three views and populations discussed above, to define the trail to the peak.

The offset hypothesis

The offset hypothesis designates the tendency in some languages for non-natives to understand more than they are able to say. The Foreign Service Institute calls this the "comprehension advantage" (Stevick, 56, p. 89). A striking example of offset occurred in an Arabic test. The candidate could barely order a cup of coffee (Speaking Level 0/0+) but understood high-level Arabic news broadcasts (Understanding Level 4).

A noticeable offset is predictable at all but the lowest levels following Krashen's input hypothesis (Krashen, 33, pp. 51–66; details in Long, 37). How extensive? At what levels such divergencies manifest themselves bears investigation. Do the levels in government differ from those in academia? If so, what accounts for the differences? In proficiency terms, the offset hypothesis suggests that listening comprehension will exceed speaking proficiency by some measurable amount, such as a plus point. The following data are based on performance of adult government employees (aged eighteen and older) who participated in intensive courses (six months for French or Spanish; one year for Vietnamese; two years—with one of the years in the target language country—for Arabic, Chinese, Japanese, or Korean).

Spanish patterns. First, 218 randomly selected ILR Spanish tests were examined. (See Table 1.) Each sheet contained a speaking score and a listening comprehension score. In Spanish the listening comprehension score is assigned on the basis of the exchange between OPI testers and the candidate, with no special added section to test listening. But experienced testers probe to raise the level of speaking *and* to test understanding.

Despite the lack of a thorough listening comprehension test supplementing the interview, raters marked the sheets with a listening score (Tables 2 and 3):

Table 1. Spanish S-Scores (N=218)

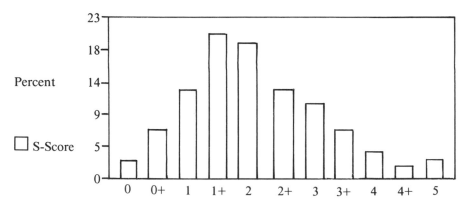

Percent

☐ S-Score

S-Levels

- lower than the speaking score 0 percent of the time (negative offset)
- equal to the speaking score 24 percent of the time (no offset)
- higher than the speaking score 76 percent of the time (positive offset).

In sum, *over 75 percent of the Spanish tests reveal the offset.* A further question: Did ascertainable differences emerge by level? Yes. A very specific and puzzling pattern emerged. The divergence tended to be strongest at Levels 2 through 4+ where the range of differences extended from a plus point to two whole points (see Table 2). At Levels 1+ and lower, however, the scores (listening and speaking) tended to be equal (see Table 4). The pattern is puzzling, because if Krashen is right about listening as a prerequisite for speaking, then one would expect the offset to appear almost immediately—if not at speaking Level 0, then at least by speaking Level 0+. But the offset seems to begin later.

Moreover, the data reveal the offset without a specific test for listening comprehension. The question arises whether a supplementary listening comprehension test would confirm the trends identified in the Spanish sample.

Confirmation from French. To ascertain whether the Spanish trends were language-specific or an artifact of the OPI as used by Spanish testers, a similar study was conducted for French ratings. A modification was introduced so that listening comprehension was expressly tested by the testers reading aloud suitable listening comprehension passages to the candidate, who then summarized them in English at the lower and mid levels and who was free but not required to paraphrase them in the target language at the higher levels (Level 4 and above).

The French data reflect patterns in 299 randomly selected interviews, each supplemented by a listening comprehension test administered directly after the oral part concluded. The Spanish trends were confirmed, but the percentages differed slightly. The data showed French listening comprehension (see Table 3):

- lower than speaking less than 1 percent of the time (negative offset)
- equal to speaking 52 percent of the time (no offset)
- higher than speaking 47 percent of the time (positive offset).

While not matching the Spanish percentages, the French data suggest that a large number of candidates in French exist whose listening comprehension exceeds their speaking ability by measurable amounts. The range, one level to one level and a plus level, however, proved slightly smaller than in Spanish (see Table 4), perhaps due to the more stringent testing method:

- 32 percent of the total interviews examined were a plus level higher
- 11 percent were a full level higher
- 1 percent were a level and a plus level higher
- 0 percent were at two full levels higher.

Table 2. Spanish Speaking (S) and
Understanding (U) Scores Compared (*N*=218)

Speaking Level	Number of Cases	UNDERSTANDING		
		U less than S	U ='S S	U greater than S
S-0	7	–	6	1
S-0+	12	–	7	5
S-1	28	–	15	13
S-1+	44	–	6	38
S-2	42	–	6	36
S-2+	29	–	4	26
S-3	25	–	4	21
S-3+	13	–	–	13
S-4	8	–	–	8
S-4+	4	–	–	4
S-5	6	–	6	3

Table 3. Relation of U-Score to S-Score

Relation	Spanish	French
Lower (negative offset)	0%	1%
Equal (no offset)	24%	52%
Higher (positive offset)	76%	47%
N ='S	218	299

Table 4. Magnitude of Offset

Magnitude	Spanish	French
Plus point lower	–	1%
Plus point higher	46%	34%
A full point higher	24%	12%
A point and a half higher	5%	1%
Two full points higher	less than 1%	–
Percentages of *N*:	76%	48% (47 higher + 1 lower)

Table 5. Distribution of French Speaking Scores (N=299)

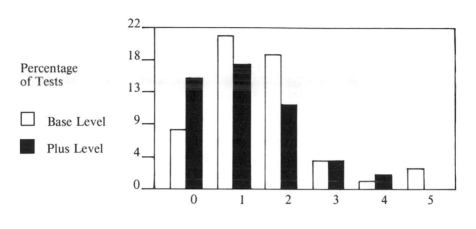

ILR Level

**Table 6. Breakdown of Spanish Understanding and
Speaking Scores by Magnitude of Difference**

		Difference		
Levels	+	1	1+	2
S-0	1	–	–	–
S-0+	5	–	–	–
S-1	12	–	–	–
S-1+	29	–	–	–
S-2	17	7	2	–
S-2+	6	13	3	–
S-3	11	9	1	2
S-3+	8	14	5	–
S-4	1	6	–	–
S-4+	4	–	–	–
S-5	–	–	–	–

The French and Spanish figures suggest that the listening comprehension level can differ markedly from speaking. The combined French and Spanish data reveal a positive offset in about 60 percent of the texts. The data, therefore, strongly suggest that listening comprehension deserves to be tested separately to ascertain the extent of the difference.

The point at which the offset began in French differed from that of Spanish. In the French tests the offset began sooner, at the Level 0+/1 border, as we had hypothesized originally for Spanish. We hazard an explanation. Perhaps, assessing the level at which the offset begins to play a significant role requires more refined listening comprehension instruments such as the supplementary passages with oral summary, recorded passages with multiple-choice items, or other approaches more finely tuned than the OPI alone.

The negative offset hypothesis

Does the comprehension advantage exist in every language? In which language is it neutral or even negative?

Surprisingly, one possible offset is *negative*. Candidates are able to speak the target language at a higher level than they can understand it. Early in our work, we became aware that listening comprehension scores in some languages sometimes patterned another way. The Spanish data brought no such cases. But in the French data, 1 percent of the time the offset proved negative. Hearing deficiency, of course, is its most obvious possible cause.

While negative offsets occur less often in Whorf's Standard Average European languages, in certain languages ILR instructors perceive a negative offset with some regularity. One candidate in Vietnamese (a tone language) spoke at Level 1+ but failed to comprehend many of the testers' utterances at the same level. He understood at a lower level than he spoke—a negative offset.

To determine the prevalence of negative offset, data must be gathered from languages markedly different in structure, lexicon, and culture from Standard Average European. One can put forth a number of reasons to explain this phenomenon. Comprehension in Standard Average European languages may be furthered by several commonalities with English: worldview, Greco-Roman-Romance vocabulary, language structures, etc. Obviously, comprehension for American English speakers will be hindered where the target language lacks such commonalities. Furthermore, languages possessing standard versions with rapid speech delivery (even Standard Average European languages such as French); languages possessing short and long consonant distinctions (Finnish) and/or short, half-long, and long vowel distinctions (Japanese); and languages with tones (Chinese), represent blocks to rapid comprehension for native American English speakers.

A final contributor may simply be lack of exposure due to unavailability of speakers and materials. Comprehension requires exposure. Exposure to a language like Vietnamese is hard to come by when only one teacher and only one text and accompanying tape set are available. In more commonly taught languages like Spanish, one language laboratory we know has seventeen sets of taped materials in addition to the tapes for the class text. Such availability increases exposure exponentially.

A study needs to be conducted to identify which languages reflect a different relationship between speaking and listening. How many languages would belong to this group? Experience to date suggests as candidates Arabic, Chinese, Japanese, Korean, Thai, and Vietnamese—all languages culturally and structurally very different from English. But this group could conceivably be expanded to include languages from Africa and India.

The data on the negative offset prove inconclusive. (See Tables 7 and 8.) Data in five languages (Arabic, Mandarin Chinese, Japanese, Korean, and Vietnamese) on randomly selected rating sheets for a total of 220 interviews were examined. Since the ns per single language were small, the totals for all five were analyzed together. These data do not reveal a negative offset. Yet many experienced ILR instructors and testers continue to feel that it exists (Rickerson, 53). What could account for indeterminacy in the data?

Reexamining the French data proves informative. In French (based on

Table 7. Non-Standard Average European Languages
Negative Offset Data

Lower (negative offset)	0
Equal (no offset)	172
Higher (positive offset)	48
Total Tests:	220

Table 8. Non-SAE-Test S-Score Distribution by Level

Level	Number of Cases	Level	Number of Cases
5	23	2+	19
4+	6	2	27
4	13	1+	16
3+	14	1	27
3	14	0+	53
		0	8
		Total Tests:	220

an *n* of 299), the offset appeared in only 1 percent of the cases; but compared to Spanish, the offset appeared only when a more fine-grained listening comprehension procedure was employed.

In the non-Standard Average European languages discussed here, testers do not employ a supplementary listening comprehension test procedure. Moreover, the combined *n*s for these languages total only a little over two-thirds of the French *n*. As a result we can probably say that the negative offset does not represent a major pattern in the non-Standard Average European test data examined here. *The data, however, do not disprove a negative offset but rather indicate insufficient proof of its existence.*

Unfortunately, tests in these languages occur so infrequently that gathering data is slow and arduous. If sufficient data can be collected, we hazard the guess that the negative offset may emerge not as a major but as a minor pattern indicative of lower than of mid or higher levels. Introduction of a more precise procedure for evaluating listening comprehension in these languages and subsequent data collection is indicated.

We turn now from data-supported to experience-supported hypotheses.

The cultural integration hypothesis for Standard Average European languages

"When will students learn that culture plays as big a role as language? My best student just did a role play. Over lunch he was to discuss a business matter with one of my countrymen. But he forgot that in my country *business comes after dessert.*" Culture, obviously, plays an important role in human exchanges. In foreign language exchanges the target language speaker expects one approach, the lower-level nonnative speaker often employs another. The result is miscommunication, discomfort, or both.

The government has long been interested in the point at which adult government foreign language learners express themselves automatically in culturally appropriate ways. ILR experience leads to the cultural integration hypothesis: Americans speaking Standard Average European languages integrate culture starting at Level 3, rarely earlier. By culture we mean the "small c" variety, that which is expressed through language. Examples are: apologizing in a suitable target language rather than English manner; accepting a compliment on one's clothes, not by saying "Thank you" (American English), but by demurring suitably in the target language—"Oh, I've had it a while," if this is culturally appropriate. Data are being gathered on this point.

The cultural integration hypothesis for non-Standard Average European languages

Do languages that are structurally and culturally very different from English require a learner to use culture earlier? As in listening, government experience suggests that languages like Chinese, Japanese, Thai, and Vietnamese differ from Standard Average European languages in regard to integrating culture. Apparently languages other than the Standard Average European require an earlier integration of culture. Suitable data are being gathered.

In proposing these two related hypotheses on integrating culture, we are aware that the government's approach to teaching culture may influence the integration point. At some government agencies, such as the Foreign Service Institute, students attend a concurrent, separate culture course, whereas at other agencies culture is integrated into the language course itself. The FSI is currently experimenting with a culture block to be inserted directly into target language instruction.

Perhaps earlier emphasis on culture in Standard Average European courses would lead to earlier integration, as suggested by Lange and Crawford-Lange (34), who stress process rather than content. We hazard a guess as to the reason for the current situation in Standard Average European language performances: up to Level 3 the monitor overloads with lexical, grammatical, and phonetic information. Consequently, integration of culture tends to come at Level 3 or later.

Earlier acquisition of culture is demonstrated by non-Standard Average European language courses in which students are forced to integrate it sooner. This phenomenon appears in courses for languages as divergent from English as Chinese, Japanese, Thai, and Vietnamese, when natives hear Americans attempting to use the target language and are more confused than amused by the intrusion of American cultural patterns. The confusion leads to students integrating the cultural component around Level 2. Is it coincidence that these languages take longer to acquire than French and Spanish? Is the need to learn culture earlier the culprit? Rather than having a possible inhibitory effect, could culture affect acquisition synergistically? One possible study would ascertain whether the earlier introduction of culture, in any way, accelerates or retards attainment of the next higher levels. Such data would be welcome.

The accelerated output hypothesis

Output is used here in a positive sense. Nowhere does current language-acquisition theory à la Krashen and the government differ more visibly than in the rather widespread government belief that one can begin to practice speaking the first day. Because government language courses often achieve results in the mid ranges (1+, 2, 2+, 3), something demonstrably different pedagogically must be taking place. Time-on-task, aptitude, motivation have all been cited as contributors. Concentration on functional foreign language, exposure to native instructors, hearing more of the language, getting more practice are other factors. The variables are legion; the data insufficient; the unknowns perhaps not currently identifiable. Yet, something different is happening.

Before proceeding we must cite what we believe to be a crucial similarity between a Krashen-type academic program and a government intensive one: *input + 1*; that is, comprehensible input. The good government and the good academic courses share this feature. In our experience, government teachers rarely resort to "Me Tarzan, you Jane," but rather they modify within acceptable target language parameters, adjusting vocabulary to include cognates initially (in French, Spanish, German) and using simpler yet always acceptable target language syntax. These teachers purposely avoid interlanguage. (On "teacher talk" and its manifestations, see Hatch, 22.)

In at least one government language school, teachers are trained to speak, however simply, within normal target language fluency ranges (no slower than a target language native would). Such training in listening comprehension at normal speed may also account for differing speaking and comprehension ratings. An important question to be researched: "Which variables contribute most to successful attainment of proficiency?" One plausible combination includes input + 1 and time-on-task as the two major factors. However, other combinations are possible and should be examined in a research setting.

A government student will normally emerge from a six-month Spanish course in the 1+ to 2+ range. Since the government grades languages by difficulty and therefore adjusts course length, the same general results require almost eight months in German, one year in Russian, and two years in Arabic, Chinese, Japanese, and Korean (with the second year in a target language country). Highly motivated or gifted students, then, *do* achieve Level 3. Unfortunately we lack solid time-to-proficiency data. Even if such data became available, however, variables intervene that complicate predicting how a given individual will do in a particular language. Our experience suggests that classes progress rather uniformly to the 0+/1 border and that individual differences due to aptitude, motivation, learning style, and learning pace emerge (if they have not already done so) in the 1/1+ ranges and definitely play a role from then on. Moreover students in these ranges reach plateaus of varying duration. One case we know of reached a plateau that lasted for two years. He did indeed learn the target language, but his department wanted to send him abroad after six months. Some plateaus last too long for the training time available.

The numerous variables complicate the selection of any single one variable (the desired research technique). Instead we posit a constellation of factors. For future investigations we select precisely those attributes of government language courses diverging from current theory. We assert that directed speaking practice from day one works; that intelligent adults can and do successfully modify their output through conscious derivation, learning, and application of rules; that after the initial stages the affective filter hardly plays an *inhibiting* role (see above). Three roles for the filter may be distinguished: *inhibitory, neutral, facilitating.* At the foot, the filter inhibits, unless tended to; at the base camp and peak, it proves neutral— that is, it rarely inhibits. Foreign Service Institute work currently in progress suggests that attending to the filter can play a *facilitating* role in classroom teaching from the lowest levels upward into Level 4 (see Ehrman, 21). These are strong statements. We hope they prove testable. These hypotheses need not be perfectly or elegantly stated or ultimately proven right. Yet, particularly striking differences between learner outcomes in academia and those in government should be highlighted and investigated, and the body of knowledge about how languages are acquired/learned be enriched.

Obviously we must mount a research effort both within and without the government. To this end the ACTFL/ETS/ILR proficiency scale can provide the vital link. The scale furnishes a common metric for studies conducted in academia, government, and business. For now we must be content to cite the discrepancy between what the government produces and how it produces it on the one hand, and the claims of current theory about how such proficiency should be acquired on the other. Studies are definitely indicated.

The immersion integration hypothesis

Not only do government language programs differ from academic ones in focus, length, and intensity, but also in techniques. Probably the most striking technique originally based on the Middlebury Summer Schools is immersion. Like several other terms in the government, *immersion* means something different than it does in academia. The government use corresponds most to academia's "intensive" language programs. Government immersion exists in short ("mini-immersion") courses lasting two and a half days with eating, drinking, and talking the target language and a longer version ("maxi-immersion") which ranges from two weeks to a month. These programs encourage the candidate to use *functional foreign language.* In the longer programs some grammar and vocabulary review takes place. But the course stresses language use with suitable practice in everyday situations and helpful guidance in how to acquire the language. As originally conceived, government maxi-immersion was designed to take Level 2/2+ students across the Level 2+/3 border. Since acquisition difficulty and consequently, the ILR scale, grow exponentially (see Figure 3 above), this goal is hard to achieve. Government maxi-immersion succeeds in producing a small number of Level 3s. Two questions immediately spring to mind: Why do so few successful 2/2+ students cross the 3 border and what happens to those maxi-immersion participants even lower on the scale? We address the latter question.

Here we must offer experiential rather than empirical data. We hypothesize that a *readiness threshold* exists. Below this threshold government students usually fail to benefit from maxi-immersion. Why? To profit from the experience, a participant must have a suitable base in vocabulary and grammar and a suitable set of strategies for acquiring and integrating more of each into his emerging target language system, *as well as* suitable feedback from native speakers (or higher-level nonnative speakers of the language) to deter fossilization. Lacking these skills, a student in an immersion program flounders and drowns.

Based on small numbers, ILR experience suggests that such floundering occurs at Level 1+ or lower. To profit from the maxi-immersion experience at all, participants at Level 1+ and lower require special sessions and special materials. General target language television programs and movies shown to all participants generally exceed Level 1/1+ students' comprehension abilities. Yet these programs present precisely the types of language they would encounter in the target language country. Higgs and Clifford (23) discuss other ramifications of this problem: the i + X problem (language beyond the student's independent level of functioning) may lead him to usage of incorrect forms, to fossilization, to what we call elsewhere the "street" and, in its most extreme form, the "terminal 1+" or "terminal 2+" syndrome. Similarly, 0+ proves too low a level for mini-immersion. If the government has found that levels exist for which both mini- and maxi-immersion prove unprofitable, what does that say about curriculum design within and without the government? Again, ILR experience offers a partial answer: the mini-immersion programs whet the participant's appetite, coming as they do at the 1/1+ border. The maxi-immersion programs prove less effective if they come too early, say, before the 2 border.

We have proceeded from hypotheses verifiable by data to those hypotheses whose existence reflects government experience and which must still be investigated empirically. Our purpose is not to prove every single hypothesis, though given the type of work we do and the kinds of learners we teach, such hypotheses appear plausible. What will we have learned about these hypotheses in the next five years? Will they be confirmed? Modified? Rejected? Will the proficiency scale have helped? What will foot-of-the-mountain researchers have contributed to our understanding of the base-camp speaker? And what insights will peak scalers provide? Using the ILR scale we can integrate our efforts.

Life at the Peak (Level 5)—Some Comments on the Educated Native Speaker (ENS)

Throughout this chapter we have discussed the dynamic nature of the ILR proficiency scale, its adaptability and suitability as a common metric for discussing both government and academic learner outcomes, and as a synthesizing principle in language acquisition research. We alluded to the criterion referenced nature of the system but said little about the well-educated native speaker. The phrase, *well-educated native speaker* derives from Oskarsson's adaptation of the ILR system to Sweden (50). The term also fits the American context, where education is widespread so that many qualify as educated, even though they might not have been exposed to a sufficiently wide range of language or might not consciously choose to reflect Level 5 in their speech, writing, etc. (e.g., American politicians for whom sounding like an "egghead" is anathema). The concept is key because all performances are compared to what an ENS would do (say, understand, read, or write) in the same situation, and the nonnative performance is rated on how closely it approximates an ENS's communicative power, style, and accuracy.

Historically, the ENS became the ultimate criterion because the Department of State needed high-level language skills for diplomatic work, even extending to skills such as negotiation and treaty writing. Had this not been so, many users today agree that the reference point could have been simply the native speaker (NS). In everyday life we tend to speak at Level 3, with forays into higher levels, as required for technical topics. The system could, therefore, have stopped at Level 3 or at the most Level 4, the highest level normally attained by nonnatives. The ACTFL/ETS guidelines chose wisely to terminate at Level 3/Superior for many of the same reasons.

Despite its utility, the ENS concept is worrisome. The concept seems to fly in the face of American egalitarianism. Yet the ILR Testing Committee's experience suggests that while there may be much disagreement at times about the nature of the ENS, there is still more disagreement about the NS. The latter is the broader concept. As a result, defining it is harder. The situation is analogous to judging wines in general or to judging the highest grade wine (*appellation controlée, Qualitätswein mit Prädikat*). Some who claim to sell "wine" object to the higher criterion. But if a criterion shift occurs, then defining the broader criterion proves more difficult: Is "Zeller Schwarze Katz" a quality wine? Is "Bernkastler Doktor und Graben" a quality wine? The narrower criterion works. Linguistically, the narrower criterion also works. Most languages have a clearly identifiable group that natives, from the man on the street to a member of the group, recognize as an educated native speaker.

Acquisition of ENS status requires long-term familiarization with varying kinds of language from everyday to formal, over a wide number of both concrete and abstract subject areas, and with varying social groups. In countries with formal educational systems, most speakers attain ENS status through learning to use the native language in a wide variety of settings offered by home and school. The scale is developmental in nature; it is not an acquisition scale per se (see Lowe, 47). In fact, the task universals cited may be defined circularly, i.e., the original needs analysis identified them as required at specific levels and, as a result, they are now required at those levels. Acquiring the scale fully seems to demand about twenty-one to twenty-four years: from mother's knee through a college education in the U.S.; lycée, Gymnasium in Europe; university in Latin America. Suitable educational sequences can be found for most languages and cultures. Possessing a diploma does not mark the ENS, though most have one. Speaking like an ENS *does* so mark him or her. Reference to "stratified" societies (Britain, France, Germany) makes the ENS concept more readily accessible. Due to social leveling, American English does not constitute a good reference point. Research efforts, we believe, demand the narrower, more easily definable criterion.

Space precludes discussion of what the foot of the mountain and the base camp look like to the ENS or to those who have come close to that designation. Even in a target language country the educated native speakers do not constitute a majority. The statistical mode would most likely be Level 3. And the percentage of nonnatives equivalent to the ENS is miniscule; the number met in ten years of testing thousands constitutes less than 1 percent of the total tested. The number of students at Level 3+, 4, and 4+ proves only somewhat larger compared with the lower levels where the preponderance of language learners exist. Few higher-level learners discuss their experiences. Fewer still keep notes on them. But such people exist. One learner we know rates Level 3, 3+, or 4 in four major languages—French, German, Russian, and Spanish. Another can order a cup of coffee in seven languages, with speaking skills ranging from Levels 0+ through 2 in most; through Levels 2+ to 3 in a couple; and to Levels 3+, 4 in the best two. Another rates Level 4+ in German, Level 3+ in Chinese, and Level 1 in Swedish. These learners should record their language-learning experiences. What does the view from just below the peak look like? They could tell us.

Toward Synthesis

We have seen that the hypotheses and data, both empirical and experiential, may be viewed from several different vantage points. Viewed from the foot of the mountain, they may prove contradictory. Viewed from the base camp, they may appear significant. Viewed from the top of the mountain, they may no longer be entirely visible. It takes the full climb and a memory of the paths trodden to begin to integrate the broader language-acquisition picture.

We foresee a period of readjustment as each view assimilates the other's hypotheses, data, and experiences. It is in the nature of theoretical systems that once a theoretical framework has been established the integration of new data still requires both time and rethinking of the framework. This realignment will doubtless be true for all three views. This chapter suggests that by employing proficiency as both a common metric and as a synthesizing research principle this process will take us further along the trail up the mountain.

Our focus above centers primarily on base-camp hypotheses, data, and experience. That focus results from the conviction that it is precisely here that government foreign language programs can make a unique contribution to learning in schools. Needless to say, base-camp hypotheses do not invalidate foot-of-the-mountain data. But base-camp hypotheses do require the reintegration and reformulation of foot-of-the-mountain hypotheses. And vice versa. Thus, we enter an *un*easy period. The birth of new insights repays the effort.

Conclusion

Many mountains exist in the range of human experience. If our world is dominated by the Language Acquisition Mountain, that is because it is our chosen field. But another mountain looms in the range, the mountain from which the government views the national need for various skills. The view from the National Need Mountain requires, as Child (10, 11) proposes, the integration of our various views. It requires a usable product to promote international commerce, diplomacy, cultural exchange, and our national security. The national need demands speakers, understanders, readers, and writers with functional foreign language skills and a better understanding of how to produce them. Adopting proficiency as a synthesizing research principle moves us toward a fuller understanding of language acquisition and, therefore, ultimately moves the nation toward producing better foreign language learners to meet the national need.

References, The ILR Proficiency Scale as a Synthesizing Research Principle: The View from the Mountain

1. Adams, Marianne Lehr, and David Argoff. "FSI's Revised Performance Standards: Assessing Communicative Effectiveness," in James R. Frith and Judith E. Liskin-Gasparro, eds., *Measuring Spoken Language Proficiency,* vol. 2. Papers from the 1981, 1982, 1983 presessions sponsored by Georgetown University Language Round Table on Languages and Linguistics and U.S. Government Interagency Language Roundtable. Washington, DC: Georgetown University, forthcoming.
2. Allen, Elissa Natelson. *The Predictive Validity of Each of the Five Parts of the Modern Language Aptitude Test: The Effect of Previous Language Training on MLAT Scores; The Correlation of MLAT Scores and Achievement in Specific*

Language Groups. Ph.D. Dissertation. Washington, DC: Georgetown University, 1976.

3. Bachmann, Lyle F., and Adrian S. Palmer. "The Construct Validation of the FSI Oral Interview." *Language Learning* 31, 1 (June 1981):67–86.

4. Buck, Kathryn A. "Nurturing the Hothouse Special." *Die Unterrichtspraxis* 17, 2 (Fall 1984): forthcoming.

5. Byrnes, Heidi. "Some Implications of Recent Research in Listening Comprehension." Symposium on Receptive Skills, sponsored by the National Security Agency and The American Council on the Teaching of Foreign Languages, held at the Defense Language Institute, Monterey, California, November 28–30, 1983. *Foreign Language Annals* 17, 2 (September 1984):317–29.

6. Canale, Michael. "Considerations in the Testing of Reading and Listening Proficiency." Symposium on Receptive Skills, sponsored by the National Security Agency and The American Council on the Teaching of Foreign Languages, held at the Defense Language Institute, Monterey, California, November 28–30, 1983. *Foreign Language Annals* 17, 2 (September 1984): 349–57.

7. _____, and Merrill Swain. "Communicative Approaches to Second Language Teaching and Testing." *Applied Linguistics* 1 (Spring 1980):1–47.

8. Carroll, John B., et al. *The Foreign Language Attainments of Language Majors in the Senior Year: A Survey Conducted in U.S. Colleges and Universities.* Cambridge, MA: Graduate School of Education, Harvard University, 1967. [EDRS: ED 013 343.]

9. _____. "The Psychology of Language Testing," pp. 46–49 in Alan Davies, ed., *Language Testing Symposium.* London: Oxford University Press, 1968.

10. Child, James. "Language Proficiency and the Typology of Tests," in James R. Frith and Judith E. Liskin-Gasparro, eds., *Measuring Spoken Language Proficiency,* vol. 2. Papers from the 1981, 1982, 1983 presessions sponsored by Georgetown University Language Round Table on Languages and Linguistics and U.S. Government Interagency Language Roundtable. Washington, DC: Georgetown University, forthcoming.

11. _____. "Measuring Language Learner Performance against a Model of Native Speaker Competence," in Martha Herzog, ed., *Pre-GURT Proceedings 1984.* Papers from the 1984 presession sponsored by Georgetown University Language Round Table on Languages and Linguistics and U.S. Government Interagency Language Roundtable. Monterey, CA: Defense Language Institute Foreign Language Center, forthcoming.

12. Clark, John L. D. *Foreign Language Testing: Theory to Practice.* Philadelphia: The Center for Curriculum Development, 1972. (Available from Didier, 29 Lexington Road, Concord, MA.)

13. _____. Personal communication.

14. Clifford, Ray T. "FSI Factor Scores and Global Ratings," pp. 27–30 in James R. Frith, ed., *Measuring Spoken Language Proficiency.* Papers from the 1980 presession sponsored by Georgetown University Language Round Table on Languages and Linguistics and U.S. Government Interagency Language Roundtable. Washington, DC: Georgetown University, 1980.

15. _____. "Oral Proficiency Performance Profiles and Global Ratings," in James R. Frith and Judith E. Liskin-Gasparro, eds., *Measuring Spoken Language Proficiency,* vol. 2. Papers from the 1981, 1982, 1983 presessions sponsored by Georgetown University Language Round Table on Languages and Linguistics and U.S. Government Interagency Language Roundtable. Washington, DC: Georgetown University, forthcoming.

16. _____. "Testing Oral Language Proficiency: A Dynamic Model." Paper presented at the Second Language Testing Symposium of the Interuniversitaere

Sprachtestgruppe, Darmstadt, Germany, May 1980. Also see in Christine Klein-Braley and Douglas K. Stevenson, eds., *Practice and Problems in Language Testing 2.* Frankfurt am Main, Federal Republic of Germany: Verlag Peter D. Lang, forthcoming.

17. _____. Personal communication.

18. _____, and Pardee Lowe, Jr. *Functional Trisection of Oral Proficiency.* Washington, DC: The Central Intelligence Agency, 1980.

19. _____, Martha Herzog, and Pardee Lowe, Jr. *Functional Quintasection of Reading Proficiency.* Monterey, CA: The Defense Language Institute Foreign Language Center, 1982.

20. Coste, D., et al. *Un niveau-seuil.* Strasbourg: Council of Europe, 1976.

21. Ehrman, Madeline. "Helping Students Take Advantage of Rich and Real Context." Paper read at a preconference workshop sponsored by Georgetown University Language Round Table on Languages and Linguistics and U.S. Government Interagency Language Roundtable. Washington, DC: Georgetown University, 1984.

22. Hatch, Evelyn. "Simplified Input and Second Language Acquisition," pp. 64–86 in Roger Andersen, ed., *Pidginization and Creolization as Language Acquisition.* Rowley, MA: Newbury House, 1983.

23. Higgs, Theodore V., and Ray T. Clifford. "The Push Toward Communication," pp. 57–79 in Theodore V. Higgs, ed., *Curriculum, Competence, and the Foreign Language Teacher.* The ACTFL Foreign Language Education Series, vol. 13. Lincolnwood, IL: National Textbook Company, 1982.

24. Hinofotis, Frances B.; John Schumann; Mary McGroarty; Melinda Erickson; Thom Hudson; Linda Kimbell; Mary Lee Scott. "Relating FSI Oral Interview Scores to Grammatical Analyses of the Learner's Speech." Paper prepared for the LS/DLI Oral Interview Project. n.d.

25. Hughes, Arthur, and Don Porter. *Current Developments in Language Testing.* New York: Academic Press, 1983.

26. Hymes, Dell. "On Communicative Competence," in J. B. Pride and J. Holmes, eds., *Sociolinguistics.* Hammandsworth, England: Penguin Books, 1972.

27. Ingram, D. E., and Elaine Wylie. *Australian Second Language Proficiency Ratings (ASLPR).* Developed under the direction of the Joint Commonwealth-States Committee on the Adult Migrant Education Program established by the Australian Department of Immigration and Ethnic Affairs, 1981.

28. Jones, Randall L. "Testing Speaking Proficiency," pp. 1–7 in Randall L. Jones and Bernard Spolsky, eds., *Testing Language Proficiency.* Arlington, VA: Center for Applied Linguistics, 1975.

29. _____. "Testing: A Vital Connection," pp. 237–65 in June K. Phillips, ed., *The Language Connection: From the Classroom to the World.* The ACTFL Foreign Language Education Series, vol. 9. Lincolnwood, IL: National Textbook Co., 1977.

30. _____. "Interview Techniques and Scoring Criteria at the Higher Proficiency Levels," pp. 89–102 in John L. D. Clark, ed., *Direct Testing of Speaking Proficiency: Theory and Application.* Proceedings of a Two-Day Conference conducted by Educational Testing Service in cooperation with the U.S. Interagency Language Roundtable and the Georgetown University Round Table on Languages and Linguistics, March 1978.

31. _____. "The Oral Interview of the Foreign Service Institute," pp. 104–15 in Bernard Spolsky, ed., *Some Major Tests.* Papers in Applied Linguistics: Advances in Language Testing Series, 1. Arlington, VA: Center for Applied Linguistics, 1979.

32. _____. "Performance Testing of Second Language Proficiency," pp. 50–57 in Eugene J. Briere and Frances B. Hinofotis, eds., *Concepts in Language*

Testing: Some Recent Studies. Washington, DC: Teachers of English to Speakers of Other Languages, 1979.
33. Krashen, Stephen D. "Applications of Psycholinguistic Research to the Classroom," pp. 51–66 in Charles J. James, ed., *Practical Applications of Research in Foreign Language Teaching.* The ACTFL Foreign Language Education Series, vol. 14. Lincolnwood, IL: National Textbook Co., 1983.
34. Lange, Dale, and Linda M. Crawford-Lange. "Doing the Unthinkable in the Second-Language Classroom: A Process for the Integration of Language and Culture," pp. 139–77 in Theodore V. Higgs, ed., *Teaching for Proficiency, the Organizing Principle.* The ACTFL Foreign Language Education Series, vol. 15. Lincolnwood, IL: National Textbook Co., 1984.
35. Larson, Jerry W., and Randall L. Jones. "Proficiency Testing for the Other Language Modalities," pp. 113–38 in Theodore V. Higgs, ed., *Teaching for Proficiency, the Organizing Principle.* The ACTFL Foreign Language Education Series, vol. 15. Lincolnwood, IL: National Textbook Co., 1984.
36. Liskin-Gasparro, Judith E. "The ACTFL Proficiency Guidelines: A Historical Perspective," pp. 11–42 in Theodore V. Higgs, ed., *Teaching for Proficiency, the Organizing Principle.* The ACTFL Foreign Language Education Series, vol. 15. Lincolnwood, IL: National Textbook Co., 1984.
37. Long, Michael. "Second Language Acquisition," in Martha Herzog, ed., *Pre-GURT Proceedings 1984.* Papers from the 1984 presession sponsored by Georgetown University Language Round Table on Languages and Linguistics and U.S. Government Interagency Language Roundtable. Monterey, CA: Defense Language Institute Foreign Language Center, forthcoming.
38. Lowe, Pardee, Jr. *Materials for Training Testers in Oral Proficiency Tests in Foreign Languages.* Washington, DC: Central Intelligence Agency Language Learning Center, mimeo, 1975. [Revised as no. 40 below and ultimately as no. 44.]
39. _____. *The Oral Proficiency Test.* Washington, DC: U.S. Government Interagency Language Roundtable, 1976.
40. _____. *Manual for LS Interview Workshops.* Washington, DC: CIA Language School, mimeo. [Rev. as *ILR Handbook on Oral Interview Testing.* Field Test Version. Washington, DC: DLI/LS Joint Oral Interview Project, mimeo, 1982.]
41. _____. "Structure of the Oral Interview and Content Validity," pp. 71–80 in Adrian S. Palmer, Peter J. M. Groot, and George A. Trosper, eds., *The Construct Validation of Tests of Communicative Competence.* Washington, DC: Teachers of English to Speakers of Other Languages, 1981.
42. _____. "The U.S. Government's Foreign Language Attrition and Maintenance Experience," pp. 176–90 in Richard D. Lambert and Barbara F. Freed, eds., *The Loss of Language Skills.* Based on a conference held May 1980 at the University of Pennsylvania. Rowley, MA: Newbury House, 1982.
43. _____. "Focus on Performance Testing: The Government's Needs." *Journal of the Chinese Language Teaching Association* 17, 3 (October 1983):63–99.
44. _____. *ILR Handbook on Oral Interview Testing.* Field Test Version. Washington, DC: DLI/LS Joint Oral Interview Project, mimeo, July 1982, Rev. 1983.
45. _____. "Gestalts, Thresholds, and the ILR Definitions," in James R. Frith and Judith E. Liskin-Gasparro, eds., *Measuring Spoken Language Proficiency,* vol. 2. Papers from the 1981, 1982, 1983 presessions sponsored by Georgetown University Language Round Table on Languages and Linguistics and U.S. Government Interagency Language Roundtable. Washington, DC: Georgetown University, forthcoming.
46. _____. "Oral Language Proficiency Testing: A Static Model." Paper present-

ed at the Second Language Testing Symposium of the Interuniversitaere Sprachtestgruppe, Darmstadt, Germany, May 1980. Also see in Christine Klein-Braley and Douglas K. Stevenson, eds., *Practice and Problems in Language Testing 2.* Frankfurt am Main, Federal Republic of Germany: Verlag Peter D. Lang, forthcoming.

47. _____. "Proficiency-Based Curriculum Design—Principles Derived from Government Experience." *Die Unterrichtspraxis* 17, 2 (Fall 1984): forthcoming.

48. _____, and Judith E. Liskin-Gasparro. *Testing Speaking Proficiency: The Oral Interview.* Washington, DC: Center for Applied Linguistics, 1982.

49. Munby, John. *Communicative Syllabus Design.* Cambridge: Cambridge University Press, 1978.

50. Oskarsson, Mats. *Approaches to Self-Assessment in Foreign Language Learning.* Oxford: Pergamon Press, 1978.

51. Phillips, June K. "Practical Implications of Recent Research in Reading." Symposium on Receptive Skills, sponsored by the National Security Agency and The American Council on the Teaching of Foreign Languages, held at the Defense Language Institute, Monterey, California, November 28–30, 1983. *Foreign Language Annals* 17, 2 (September 1984):258–96.

52. Rice, Frank A. "Language Proficiency Testing at the Foreign Service Institute." *The Linguistic Reporter.* Washington, DC: Center for Applied Linguistics, May 1959.

53. Rickerson, Earl T. "A Curriculum for Proficiency: Concepts to Build On." *Die Unterrichtspraxis* 17, 2 (Fall 1984): forthcoming.

54. Shohamy, Elana. "The Stability of Oral Proficiency Assessment in the Oral Interview Testing Procedures." *Language Learning* 33, 4 (December 1983):527–40.

55. Stevenson, Douglas K. "Foreign Language Testing: All of the Above," pp. 153–203 in Charles J. James, ed., *Practical Applications of Research in Foreign Language Teaching.* The ACTFL Foreign Language Education Series, vol. 14. Lincolnwood, IL: National Textbook Co., 1983.

56. Stevick, Earl. "Curriculum Development at the Foreign Service Institute," pp. 85-112 in Theodore V. Higgs, ed., *Teaching for Proficiency, the Organizing Principle.* The ACTFL Foreign Language Education Series, vol. 15. Lincolnwood, IL: National Textbook Co., 1984.

57. Vincent, Robert J. "Psychophysical Scaling of the Language Proficiency Interview: A Preliminary Report," pp. 229–53, 89–102 in John L. D. Clark, ed., *Direct Testing of Speaking Proficiency: Theory and Application.* Proceedings of a Two-Day Conference conducted by Educational Testing Service in cooperation with the U.S. Interagency Language Roundtable and the Georgetown University Round Table on Languages and Linguistics, March 1978.

58. Vollmer, Helmut. "The Structure of Foreign Language Competence," pp. 3–29 in Arthur Hughes and Don Porter, eds., *Current Developments in Language Testing.* New York: Academic Press, 1983.

59. Wilds, Claudia P. "The Oral Interview Test," pp. 29–44 in Randall L. Jones and Bernard Spolsky, eds., *Testing Language Proficiency.* Arlington, VA: Center for Applied Linguistics, 1975.

2

Proficiency in Practice: The Foreign Language Curriculum

Laura K. Heilenman
Isabelle M. Kaplan
Northwestern University

"After this year, will I be able to say everything in French that I can say in English?"

> Ninth-grade French I student,
> first day of class

"If you grant for a moment that the vast majority of our students satisfy the language requirement in either Spanish, French, or German, then are you satisfied that these students can do *something* with the language? Can they speak it? Understand it? Read it? Write it? I agree that proficiency need not be defined as competency for all students in all these areas; but perhaps proficiency ought to mean competency in at least one of them."

> Letter to Chair of the Committee on Language Proficiency,
> Northwestern University,
> from Associate Dean T. W. Heyck, October 22, 1981

Laura K. Heilenman (Ph.D., University of Louisville) is a Lecturer in the Department of French and Italian at Northwestern University, where she coordinates elementary language courses and supervises teaching assistants. Her publications have appeared in *Language Learning,* the *Modern Language Journal,* and the *Report of the Central States Conference on the Teaching of Foreign Languages.* She is a member of ACTFL, AATF, MLA, and TESOL.

Isabelle M. Kaplan (DES and CAPES, Université de Clermont) is a Lecturer in the Department of French and Italian at Northwestern University, where she teaches intermediate and advanced language courses and French Culture and Civilization courses. She is a member of ACTFL, Executive Council of the Chicago/Northern Illinois Chapter of AATF, IFLTA, and a member of the Achievement Test Development Committee for the College Board Program of the Educational Testing Service. She has participated in many oral proficiency familiarization workshops and in two IFLTA oral proficiency projects.

Introduction

The two questions that begin this chapter are real ones. First, they are authentic; real people asked them with real concerns and they expected real answers. Second, they address what has become a very real and central issue in foreign language education, accountability in terms of results. People—students, parents, administrators—want to know what can be expected at the end of a course of foreign language study, and they want this stated in terms that relate to language use in a real-world context. Answering their questions by handing out facsimiles of tables of contents in the guise of curricula or syllabi is no longer sufficient. There are two reasons for this, and they are both directly connected to the problems the two opening questions represent.

First, the level of proficiency suggested by what is "covered" and "tested" in foreign language classes has always been deceptive. "Doing" foods and restaurant vocabulary does not equal being able to order a real meal in a real restaurant any more than "doing" the past tense equals the ability to recount the events of yesterday. Life and language are simply more complex than that. The restaurant is either out of all the dishes that were on the vocabulary list, or what happened yesterday refuses to be reduced to the particular verbs whose past tenses were learned.

So, the answer to the first question, the one about becoming fluent in a year, is no. In the first place, years are not precise measures of proficiency in a language. Although it is possible to predict with some degree of accuracy that increasing years of language study will imply increasing ability to use that language, the relationship is not a simple, linear one. Motivation, age, actual time spent on task, how that task was defined, aptitude, teacher proficiency, and more—all constitute variables that must be entered into the equation. In the second place, what is commonly meant by *fluency* suffers from a dangerous imprecision. Without an operational definition of what it means to be fluent or, at least, a prior consensus on this matter, it is inviting disaster to promise—or to allow it to be believed—that "fluency" will be the outcome of any number of years of language study.

The second reason why structurally based tables of contents make unsatisfactory curricula derives from the preceding discussion. It is also made painfully obvious by the difficulty we have in answering the second question asked, namely, "What can students do with the language they have learned?" The issue here is one of functional ability, of what students can do with the language, and it is inadequately addressed by a curriculum whose goals are largely concerned with nouns, verbs, pronouns, days of the week, a few personalized questions, and a reader or two. The question, as asked, did not concern students' mastery of the subjunctive but rather dealt with what they could use the subjunctive for (besides passing tests, of course!). It is an embarrassing question because we have no real answer.

These issues, accountability and real-world validity, are precisely those addressed by the proficiency guidelines issued by the American Council on the Teaching of Foreign Languages (ACTFL) (1) and the Oral Proficiency Interview with its associated rating scale developed by ACTFL and the Educational Testing Service (ETS). The centrality of these issues and the need felt by foreign language educators to come to grips with them have been attested to by the continued interest and support they have evoked. The idea of "proficiency as an organizing principle" (Higgs, 8) represents the potential for professional consensus along with the possibility of communicating, in terms that make sense to the public at large, what realistically can be expected from a given number of years of language study (Liskin-Gasparro and Woodford, 22).

The work done thus far has been detailed elsewhere (Lee, 21). This chapter is concerned with what happens next. Can we go from rating scales and proficiency guidelines to classrooms to curricula, and if so, how? The rating scale is familiar; the proficiency guidelines known; and we have some idea of what proficiency-based classrooms (Omaggio, 25), materials (Bragger, see Chapter 3), and evaluation schema (Magnan, see Chapter 4) might look like. But what about a curriculum? On what premises would it be based? What kind of instructional sequences might evolve? What would be the relationship between beginning and advanced classes? Between elementary, secondary, and postsecondary institutions? Where do we start?

We start by defining terms. The word *curriculum,* as commonly used, refers to a course of study and is primarily concerned with issues of course content, sequence, and articulation. In this sense, a foreign language curriculum can be identified with a foreign language program or course of study. Decisions made about the curriculum or program are based on assumptions regarding what should be learned (subject matter), how it should be taught (method), and the way in which successful learning should be defined (objectives, course prerequisites, exams, grades, degrees). These assumptions are also part of the curriculum but have more in common with what is usually termed approach or philosophy than with the program per se. Before attempting, then, to sketch out a proficiency-based curriculum, it is necessary to examine the assumptions or premises involved.

The Proficiency-Based Curriculum: Premises _____

1. *A proficiency-based curriculum is not identical to a set of proficiency guidelines.* Proficiency guidelines are evaluative in nature and have evolved in order to distinguish among people, not in order to instruct them. As such, they tend to focus on learner deficiencies and to be stated in negative terms (Trim, 30). Although learners at the Intermediate Level are

accurately described as producing a majority of utterances containing "fractured syntax and other grammatical errors" and using a vocabulary that is "inadequate to express anything but the most elementary needs," it is doubtful that any teacher or student would be willing to work toward that description as a goal.

A proficiency-based curriculum, then, has to identify positive if limited competencies that will constitute interim objectives, while not losing sight of the overall goal of proficiency at defined levels. At the same time, instructors must keep in mind that the descriptions embodied in the proficiency guidelines are valid. In terms of proficiency, learners, particularly at the Novice and Intermediate levels, are more accurately characterized by what they are incapable of doing than by what they succeed in doing. In terms of achievement, however, the opposite is true since achievement tests are set up to measure a discrete amount of learning in a controlled setting. Thus, one of the real challenges involved in setting up a proficiency-based curriculum lies in setting up achievement goals that lead to proficiency outcomes. (See Magnan, Chapter 4.)

2. *Proficiency in a foreign language is attained through a proficiency-based curriculum.* At first glance, this premise appears to be an obvious tautology. In the sense that the proficiency guidelines and the Oral Proficiency Interview are being used as both evaluative criteria and curricular guidelines, then the fact that what is being taught is what is expected to be learned is not terribly interesting. Interesting or not, however, this is exactly the nub of the problem in the majority of foreign language curricula. The assumption seems to have been that learning a foreign language equals learning that language's structure, along with a generous amount of vocabulary, all carefully sequenced and spooned out in judicious doses. Enough of these doses, successfully swallowed, presumably result in functional language knowledge. It sounds nice. It sounds logical. It sounds as if it should work. But it doesn't.

Learning a certain number of adjectives along with their morphological changes does not translate directly into being able to describe, just as learning the various uses and forms of the subjunctive is not the same thing as being able to defend one's opinions and state one's feelings. This is the gap that the traditional, structurally based language program has not been able to bridge regardless of the kind of methodological paraphernalia or contextualized embellishment added. The stated goal of such programs, language use, has not been met because the real goal, in terms of what students were expected to do, pertained primarily to form rather than to function and was more concerned with complete sentences than with discourse-level competence.

This was inadvertently brought out in a book-length study focusing on education in general but containing a few pages on foreign languages (Goodland, 7). In the thirteen senior high schools studied, foreign language classrooms, although occupying a very small place in the total curriculum and in the schools, impressed the researchers with their emphasis on "students doing the language," and on students being participants "in language usage" (p. 202). Equally impressive were the teachers' professed goals of "conversational fluency" and "cultural awareness" (p. 202). The tests, however, were apparently another matter. Here the stress was on the recall of specific information and "technical mastery" with very little original writing being asked for. There is no mention of oral testing (p. 202). Although many explanations are possible for the discrepancy between goals stated and the testing of students' progress toward them, it is difficult not to see this as simply another instance of double-dealing in terms of outcomes promised and goods delivered (Jorstad, 14; Lafayette and Strasheim, 18).

A proficiency-based curriculum, on the other hand, aims at global evaluation of learners' performance in the various skill areas. Proficiency is seen as a superordinate goal that represents more than the sum total of all discrete items learned and that attempts to balance accuracy with fluency and learning about a language with providing the opportunity to learn a language by using it. Furthermore, a proficiency-based curriculum specifies outcomes in terms that relate to real-world language functions and that are measurable in criterion-referenced terms that have been derived from actual learner performance.

That is to say, the goals as stated in a proficiency-based curriculum are not stated in terms of hoped-for outcomes based on assumptions about the nature of languages and the best way to go about learning them. Rather, the organization, goals, and activities of a proficiency-based curriculum are predicated on actual observations of many learners as they attempted to use the languages they were learning. In other words, a proficiency-based curriculum has its goals defined in advance. In contrast, previous attempts at curriculum building have been handicapped by having to make do with a fuzzy, if at times elegant, itinerary toward a vaguely specified destination.

3. *The demonstration of proficiency in a foreign language requires the use of the language.* Again this may seem so obvious it does not require statement. Again, however, this is so only at first glance. Students being evaluated on a proficiency basis are not well served by an ability to satisfactorily complete a grammar exercise involving question formation or the use of the imperfect in French if they cannot also ask other students where they used to live and where they went to school. It cannot be said too often that the difference between levels of proficiency as defined by the proficiency guidelines is not one of knowledge in terms of achievement tests (see Magnan, Chapter 4), but one of ability to use the language in less structured and more global settings. Intermediate-Level students, for example, may be quite capable of reciting a list of verbs that require a

subjunctive construction and may be able, given time, to provide the correct forms in a series of exercises. These same students, however, will not be able to actually use the subjunctive in discourse, for example, expressing opinions and defending points of view. That kind of ability is characteristic of Superior-Level language users whose overt knowledge of the subjunctive may well be inferior to that of Intermediate-Level students since they have, in effect, "forgotten their rules" in the process of acquiring functional control of the language.

This more or less automatic language use is one of the ultimate goals of most language programs. The assumption is that students will move from the overt manipulation of consciously learned rules to relatively automatic and accurate control of language in communicative situations. The reality is that this seldom happens, largely because students are given an overdose of knowledge about the language without a corresponding opportunity to use that language. As a result, students leave the classroom after one, two, or three years of language study with a fair amount of knowledge with regard to achievement but with only a minimal amount of ability with regard to proficiency.

A proficiency-based curriculum, on the other hand, deemphasizes the role of conscious knowledge of language rules while providing the context within which students can build the ability to use the language. Exactly how this will be done is still a matter of conjecture, although several suggestions will be made later in this chapter.

4. *Proficiency comes in three parts.* This refers, of course, to the Functional Trisection consisting of function, topic or context, and accuracy (Liskin-Gasparro, 21). The point to be made here is simple: these three components of proficiency are equally important, and curricula as well as classroom activities must be based on various combinations of them. Traditionally, curricula and classroom activities have been accuracy-driven with little if any organized thought given to function and context. A proficiency-based curriculum strives for a balance among the three, while at the same time allowing for the imbalance frequently seen at the Novice and Intermediate levels where one component may compensate for another.

5. *Proficiency objectives must be based on obtainable levels of proficiency.* There are two points to be made here. First, we simply do not know with any degree of certainty what levels of proficiency are obtainable for the majority of our students. We may have some educated guesses, based on current conditions, but we have no sure knowledge. This is, of course, an empirical question, the preliminary answers to which have been rather discouraging (Carroll, 3; Lange, 19). Relatively rapid progress can be made through the Novice Level, but a plateau may well be reached at the Intermediate Level that resists the efforts of both students and instructors.

This may be the problem underlying the difficulties encountered at the second- and even third-year level where progress seems minimal even when effort is maximal. Whether or not instructional intervention can make the transition from Intermediate to Advanced less wearing and more efficient remains to be seen.

The second point to be made is that the equation of levels of proficiency with years of study is ill-advised at best. Although the majority of students in "German I" will be Novices, little is predictable after that. A proficiency-based curriculum will not eliminate individual differences. However, it may help us to utilize them more effectively.

6. *A proficiency-based curriculum must follow the sequence of attainable levels of proficiency.* One of the most valuable contributions made by the idea of proficiency concerns the grading of language ability. Instead of the monolithic, all-or-nothing concept of "fluency" or the vagueness of "being able to do something with the language," there is a carefully delineated progression of levels moving from no functional ability in the language to an ability virtually equivalent to that of an educated native speaker.

The implications are numerous. To begin with, the existence of a range of levels restores the validity of the apprentice-learner. The description of characteristics for each level includes what can and cannot be done. While the inability to perform some functions or maintain a level of accuracy may exclude learners from a specific level, it does not exclude them from being proficient at their own level. Further there is no stigma attached to being an Advanced or an Intermediate or even a Novice. Each level represents an area of competency in which individuals may or may not choose to stay, according to their goals and priorities.

It is important, however, to keep in mind that not all levels are created equal. The levels of proficiency are ranked in a progressive order that points to a sequencing of abilities in which first things must come first. This implies that instruction should start at the Novice Level and that teaching must be geared to the proficiency requirements of that level. Only after such proficiency has been demonstrated can learners be expected to be able to function at the next level. In simplest terms, expecting students whose proficiency level is in the Intermediate range to be able to discuss plot, describe characters, and analyze style (all Advanced or Superior tasks when performed with accuracy) is equivalent to placing them in an endless state of "language breakdown." At present, this is seen most frequently at the interface between language courses and beginning literature courses, but it can occur at any point where course demands outstrip linguistic proficiency.

Finally, proficiency does not mean perfection, nor does it imply limitation of instruction to one level at a time. Although learners may be performing at one level, there will be attempts at and peaks into others. A proficiency-based curriculum must, then, provide instruction and training that looks toward the next level while working at and consolidating skills of the level learners are presently in or aiming at. In other words, instruction at each level should not simply be oriented toward full control of the structure, functions, and context of one level, but should aim at partial control as well as conceptual control of higher levels (compare Lowe, 23).

7. *A proficiency-based curriculum is eclectic. It starts with outcomes; it does not prescribe practices.* The relative contribution model (Higgs, 8) suggests that, at different levels of proficiency, various methodologies or focuses are likely to be differentially effective (pp. 5–8). Thus a primarily structural approach may be most helpful to learners attempting to move from Intermediate Mid or Intermediate High to Advanced or a functional-notional syllabus may be optimally beneficial to learners in moving from Advanced to Superior. This does not imply an exclusivity model or a one-level/one-method approach, however. Instead, it suggests a rationally based eclecticism in which instructors pick and choose among the available methods, approaches, and techniques on the basis of their effectiveness at each given level.

8. *There appear to be upper limits on the amount of functional language that can be acquired/learned under the conditions usually surrounding foreign language learning in the United States.* The major culprit here is time. Enough time is a necessary if not sufficient prerequisite to the development of any degree of proficiency in a foreign language. Unfortunately, time, in any appreciable amount, is exactly what foreign language instruction is short of. A few quick calculations make it obvious that the accomplishment of "working proficiency" (Advanced) is in all likelihood impossible given the time usually devoted to foreign language study in this country. A typical college program providing five contact hours per week for one year and three hours of contact time per week for a second, contains a total of 201 hours of instruction. According to data from the Foreign Service Institute (4), it requires 240 hours of training in small classes with an intensive format to produce a learner whose speaking proficiency is at Level 1/1+ (Intermediate).

Keeping in mind that speakers at this level are, at best, "able to satisfy most survival needs and limited social demands" and that control of the past and future is still quite problematic, it seems useless to insist that students at the end of second year be able to discuss issues of social consequence or explain character motivation in a short story. Insisting on a Superior performance with Intermediate students leads predictably to disaster. A proficiency-based curriculum, by attempting to limit the language demanded of learners to their level or a little above, prevents this kind of mismatch.

Time, although important, is not the only factor involved. Of equal importance is the limitation imposed by the relatively narrow wedge of the universe of discourse that can be provided in a classroom (Jakobovits, 12; Kramsch, 16). One instructor providing input and interacting with twenty or more students within the confines of a classroom can in no way equal the input or interactions experienced by children learning their first language or by learners who have the advantage of being immersed in the language they are learning. This is not to imply that a classroom cannot provide students with beneficial language-learning experiences; it is to say, however, that more is needed if higher levels of proficiency are targeted. At the present moment and based on our experience, it seems unlikely that levels above Advanced can be achieved by any significant number of students whose learning experience is restricted to the academic classroom (Carroll, 3).

9. *A proficiency-based curriculum is educational in a broad sense.* It is tempting to ascribe the failure of students to successfully narrate and describe in the past, present, and future (an Advanced task) to inadequacy in the areas of auxiliaries, endings, and vocabulary. At least a portion of the problem, however, may lie in the fact that competent narrating and describing is a skill that has to be developed in any language, including the first. In other words, learning how to describe, how to narrate, and how to support opinions is a cognitive skill as well as a language-specific one. For the oral skills in particular, this is a skill that is rarely the subject of conscious academic planning. There are very few first-language units or chapters or courses devoted to the effective use of oral language at any level. The net result, then, is that asking students to narrate and describe may be asking them to do in the foreign language what they could do only with difficulty in the first.

In addition, a proficiency-based curriculum does not ipso facto exclude the study of language as a system (linguistics/structure/grammar) nor the study of culture and literature through the language as a medium of instruction.

A Basic Curricular Model

A proficiency-based syllabus is central to the development of a proficiency-based curriculum. The central feature of a proficiency-based syllabus as described here is its cyclical nature. At each level, certain structures, functions, and topics are taught for *full control,* others for *partial control,* and still others for *conceptual control.* That which is taught for partial control or conceptual control at one level of proficiency will be recycled at subsequent levels where full or partial control will be the goal.

In Figure 1, *full control* represents the level of proficiency that would normally equal Novice High according to the guidelines, while *partial*

Figure 1. A Sample Proficiency-Based Curriculum for French, Novice Level

	Functions	Content Topics	Accuracy
Full Control	Making lists Memorized materials Recycling	Daily life: objects places colors dates numbers etc. Routine activities	Basic word order Numbers (e.g., 1–20) Common adjectives/adverbs Question words *je, vous*
Partial Control	Creating with language Asking/answering questions Conducting short routine conversations Describing/ narrating in present	Everyday survival: food housing work public places sports/ leisure etc. Familiar activities: work hobbies school entertainment transportation etc. Weather/time	Articles in affirmative utterance All subject pronouns Form and place of common adjectives/adverbs Numbers (e.g., 1–100) *il y a* *mon/ma/mes, votre/vos* Present tense of common regular verbs plus *être aller* *faire comprendre* *pouvoir vouloir* *savoir devoir* Near future Passé composé of common verb *ne. . .pas*
Conceptual Control	Differentiating between memorized material and creating with language	What does it mean to carry on a conversation?	Single object pronouns Partitive in negative utterances Reflexive verbs past/present Passé composé *avoir/être*

| | | Skills | | |
Comprehension	Reading	Writing	Speaking	Culture
Understanding memorized material Operating in situations aided by context	Directions Fixed phrases in: forms maps signs schedules etc.	Transcribing memorized material Supplying information on forms Listing memorized material	Surviving with learned utterances Attempting to create with language	Greeting Leave-taking Expressing wants
Listening to nonmemorized material for basic needs/social conventions Listening for specific details	Common text types: notes memos cards lists etc.	Writing short messages and simple directions Recombining words/ structures to create simple utterances	Surviving in simple situations Asking questions Discussing self Maintaining conversation Handling simple transactions	Using behavior learned for greeting buying tipping etc.
Listening for syntactical markers	Identifying written structural items	Filling in blanks	Drilling spoken forms	Discussing cultural concepts

control represents areas that are in the Intermediate range, such as asking questions and the (limited) ability to deal with the past. *Conceptual control* refers to learning about structures that are not expected to be completely controlled until the Intermediate High/Advanced levels. The past tense system is an example of a set of structures normally controlled conceptually at the Novice Level, partially at the Intermediate Level, but fully only at the Superior Level.

The principle of a cyclical syllabus based on levels of control extends to the skill areas also. At the Novice Level, for example, writing for full control would involve the recall and transcription of memorized material in the form of lists, biographical information, and dictations. Students might write down the names of colors they associate with spring, fill in a simple job application form, or write sentences describing a picture. Writing for partial control could involve students attempting to convey their own messages, perhaps in the form of a short paragraph about themselves or a postcard describing their hometown. Writing for conceptual control would then focus on discrete-point types of exercises where learners would consciously manipulate their knowledge about the language, for instance, putting verbs in sentences and endings on adjectives.

At the levels of full and conceptual control, accuracy would be stressed and expected; while at the level of partial control, fluency would be the objective. At the same time, no one task or activity is automatically limited to any one level of control. Dictation, for example, could just as easily be a Superior as a Novice task. Transcribing the text of a radio commercial might require skills normally observed at the Advanced Level, while writing down words or sentences that have been memorized is clearly within the capabilities of most Novice-Level learners.

This design would remain basically the same at all levels of proficiency. A course aimed at the development of Intermediate-Level proficiency, for example, might place Intermediate-Level requirements in the *full control* level, Intermediate High requirements at the level labelled *partial control,* and Advanced requirements under the heading of *conceptual control.* Although the vocabulary to be learned will vary from one learning environment to the next, the principle of cyclical progression based on the sequencing suggested by the Functional Trisection in terms of function, topic, and accuracy and by the relative contribution model (Higgs, 8, pp. 4–8) in terms of skill emphasis will remain.

Teaching and learning for full control

Teaching, as well as learning, for full control of the target language will involve extensive experience with a variety of activities dealing with the functions, topics, and accuracy involved at each level of proficiency and in all five skill areas (listening comprehension, reading, writing, speaking, and culture). The focus here will be on functional language use with correction of form by the teacher limited to the structural, lexical, and phonological categories targeted for full control. Language breakdown, as evidenced by lapses into the native language, expressions of inability to continue in the target language, and a tendency to grope for communication rather than to cope with it (Jones, 13, p. 241), will all constitute a clear indication that the activity in progress is beyond the full control of the learner.

Teaching and learning for partial control

The level of partial control also focuses on language use rather than on language form, but it tolerates a greater amount of inaccuracies, native-language intrusions, and groping strategies than does teaching/learning for full control. The difference between full and partial control is similar to the difference between getting around in your neighborhood and getting around in another, less familiar part of town.

In the area of listening comprehension, at the Novice Level, students might be expected to listen for the gist of a conversation or to extract essential information from the speech flow, such as a price or a time or a date. Similarly in reading, learners could be asked to deal with texts for global comprehension, or they could be required to search for specific pieces of information, such as what time a party starts (from an invitation) or when the train leaves (from a schedule) or how many people are involved (in a dialogue). This would be in contrast to what is expected at the full-control level where learners would be responsible for complete comprehension but of a limited body of material such as street signs, map conventions, and fixed phrases likely to be encountered in the target language on a daily basis (e.g., "Step to the back of the bus," "Beware of the dog," "Dead end," "Please print or type"). Other examples of activities that might be appropriate at this level can be found in Stevick (28) and Brendel (2).

Teaching and learning for conceptual control

Teaching/learning for conceptual control is the level of instruction seen in most foreign language classrooms (compare, for example, Lafayette and Strasheim, 18). Here, the focus is clearly on form, and accuracy outweighs fluency in importance. Teaching/learning for conceptual control represents the presentation of metalinguistic concepts, such as direct objects and past tenses, and provides initial practice using form-based exercises and activities. Such activities may range from pattern drills to highly contextualized exercises, but to the extent that the focus is on form rather than function, they will not be part of the activities designed to foster partial or full control of the language. Discrete-point testing and achievement-oriented testing are most appropriate within this teaching/learning level. Proficiency-oriented testing is most appropriate at the other two levels of control.

In addition, teaching and learning for conceptual control includes discussion of what a language is, of what it means to learn a language, and of the relationship between language and culture. For example, direct objects and pronouns could be examined from a discourse point of view in an attempt to discover not only what they are but also why they are and what purpose they serve. Another topic for discussion might be the difference between using memorized language and creating with language. Students could be led to discover the limitations of a memorized dialogue and to appreciate the difference between the apparent fluency of memorized speech and the less fluent nature of language being used to communicate in real time. And finally, this instructional level would provide a forum for the discussion of cultural concepts.

Culture in a proficiency-based syllabus

The teaching and learning of culture is an integral part of a proficiency-based syllabus. Culture represents the interaction of *topics, functions,* and *accuracy.* Topics refer to words and expressions. Words represent the real world both for the native-language speaker and for the target-language speaker. While the dictionary may tell us that the word *bread* represents the physical object called *pain* in French, *bread* and *pain* do not represent the same experiences that speakers of English or French have had with the particular word. Topics take these different realities into account. Functions refer to the variety of interactions among speakers. The ability to function within a culture implies entering a system of interactions quite different from those of one's native culture. Accuracy refers to the degree of approximation of the learner's (inter)actions to those normally expected within the target culture. Thus the development of accurate cultural ability cannot be separated from that of accurate linguistic ability.

Further, the three levels of teaching and learning already described apply to culture in the same way as they do to language. At the beginning levels, culture is taught through extensive use of authentic documents dealing with the topics and functions appropriate to a given level. Gradually, as learners accumulate a base of contextualized information, along with the development of more sophisticated linguistic ability, they will be able to hypothesize and discuss the pluralistic nature of a culture. This approach capitalizes on the emphasis on concrete narration and description at the Novice and Intermediate levels (i.e., is equivalent to observation and recognition of cultural instances), while at the same time, preventing oversimplification and a reduction of the study of culture to cathedrals and croissants. Culture, as a concept, would be treated at all levels. This conceptual treatment would be brief and would occur, for the most part, in response to student demand at the Novice and Intermediate levels, becoming more complex as learners' knowledge of the culture and their ability to discuss it in the target language improve.

For instance, a study of food as a topic in a Novice course would deal with a variety of French menus from restaurants, banquet menus for wedding receptions, itemized food bills of French families from different socioeconomic strata and from different parts of the Francophone world, plus descriptions of dinners served at festive occasions. This could involve various listening and reading activities as well as provide the opportunity for speaking practice. Students could then develop menus appropriate to different occasions, make lists of items necessary for food preparation, and practice ordering meals in restaurants. Activities here could involve both writing and speaking.

The result would be that students would be introduced to cultural realities without being encouraged or forced to generalize from an insufficient information base. It will be obvious that all French people do not subsist on a daily diet of snails, bread, and wine without it being said. All this could be done in the language being learned. More complex questions, raised by students, could be dealt with briefly in the native language.

At more proficient levels, the study of culture as anthropology, sociology, and history could be undertaken. This would occur after content-oriented courses at the Intermediate and Advanced levels had established sufficient information plus the linguistic proficiency to deal with this type of study in the target language.

A Proficiency-Based Foreign Language Program

A proficiency-based curricular model or syllabus, however, is but the first step. There remains the foreign language program as a whole.

Specialist versus generalist: The beginning course

A distinct separation between the specialist student and the generalist should be maintained. Given the fact that a two- or three-year foreign language sequence seems to be entrenched in the American educational system and given the fact that this sequence is the sum total of exposure to a foreign language experienced by the majority of that minority of the American population who have had experience with a foreign language, why not make the sequence self-contained? Instead of looking at the first one or two years as the beginning steps for those few who can or will stay the distance, why not acknowledge the fact that the vast majority of our students, over 80 percent (Lafayette, 17; Ryder, 27), are in these first two years and that they will not continue? What is needed is *not* a beginning language course for the handful of future specialists, but rather a specific language course aimed at the majority of students (Hye, 11).

There are several advantages to this kind of thinking. First, this general foreign language course would be geared to the average student in each institution and would cease to be a proving ground for the successful few. As Pimsleur and Struth (26) pointed out over fifteen years ago, a system whereby the minority of students have a successful language-learning experience at the expense of the majority "is as wasteful as it is undemocratic" (p. 87). Second, the goals for the general foreign language course would be more realistic and would aim at an understanding of language and culture along with a hands-on experience with the language itself.

Specifically, the goals for a generalist foreign language course of study might include:

1. The attainment of Intermediate-Level proficiency in at least one skill area with differing levels of skill development in other areas
2. An awareness of language as a complex, socially mediated system in which many factors besides verbs and vocabulary come into play
3. An introduction to the concept of culture along with some experience in dealing with cultural similarities and differences
4. An introduction to texts and other media (arts, music, film) representative of the language and culture.

Obviously, some amount of time would be spent in the students' native language dealing with concepts too complex to be discussed or presented in the target language. Not equally obvious is the fact that this would represent an upgrading rather than a diluting of current offerings. The proficiency attained by students would be real and their understanding of its limitations would be based on an understanding of some of the processes underlying language learning and acquisition. Beyond a proficiency in language, moreover, students would be presented with an intellectual experience, a substantial percentage of the real value of which would lie in "collateral learning" (Tanner and Tanner, 29, p. 38), that is, learning that goes beyond skills and information into the areas of attitude and values.

This general foreign language course should teach, above all, that it is possible for average students to obtain a certain degree of proficiency in a foreign language while, at the same time, learning more about language, communication, and culture as intellectual concepts. The ultimate effectiveness of such a course would reside in students' memories years later, in whether they would remember "Spanish II" as valuable, interesting, and worthwhile or as useless, boring, and poorly taught (Ryder, 27).

A final advantage to this approach is that we would be dealing largely with what we have; we would not be demanding an increased span of time for language study nor would we be asking for additional funding. Instead we would be working from within, producing students with a deeper understanding of what it means to learn a foreign language and better equipped, if they so choose, to tackle later specialist courses.

This is far from a novel suggestion (see, for example, Gaudiani, 6; Valdman, 31), but it may be a timely one. The foreign language curriculum has become an unwieldy accretion of knowledge, skills, and attitudes, all of which cannot be accomplished to the same degree in a one-to-two-year course sequence. Attempting to do it all has resulted only in equal underdevelopment in all areas and, most important, in a serious public relations problem.

If the views expressed in a recent editorial published in a major newspaper (Freedman, 5) are indicative of attitudes at large, then time has begun to run out. Here, foreign language study is described as "rote drill in quirky idioms and irregular verbs" plus " 'cultural appreciation'—the sampling of tacos, quiche or sauerbraten"; present efforts to revitalize foreign language education are termed "glibly ritualistic"; and the traditional two years of language study are seen as producing little in the way of real language proficiency while simultaneously producing even less in terms of intellectual content. This is not simply another attack by a monolingual journalist; this is an indictment of foreign language programs that are not worth their curricular space. He has a point. Two years of language study do not produce any real proficiency in terms of being able to use the language studied for more than basic survival and should not claim to do so. Further, it is questionable at best if any real insight into the workings of either culture or language is accomplished when both are seen as curricular add-ons rather than as central concerns. A general language course, with limited claims concerning degree of language proficiency developed along with an intellectual content that transcends the learning of rules and the tasting of tacos, could go a long way toward meeting the larger curricular needs of American education while avoiding the descent into a phrase book plus slides type of program.

Plateau courses

Another concern is providing for the plateau stages through which learners seem to pass. As progress is made up the various scales, the complexity of the functions and contexts, as well as the degree of accuracy involved, increases. Thus the time spent at each level will increase and course offerings will have to be diversified in order to avoid endless repetitions at the same level of the same course. Perhaps one of the reasons why the grammar presented in the first year has to be done again in the second year and reviewed and gone over in the third year is that the grammar presented and learned is not internalized in any useful way.

Assuming that the majority of students reach the Intermediate Mid Level at the end of two years, the passage to Intermediate High and the more critical passages into the Advanced and Superior levels may best be achieved through courses that vary in topical content (i.e., music, science, literature, civilization, history, geography, business), but have a common core of functions, contexts, and degree of accuracy as defined by the proficiency guidelines. Thus each proficiency level would contain a basic course such as that described previously. It would not be assumed, however, that this one course would be all that was needed to ensure proficiency at a given level. Instead, content courses, geared to the level involved, would be developed so that students could have the opportunity to use the language they have learned.

Presumably, courses at the Intermediate High/Advanced Level would have a descriptive/narrative focus, while courses at the Advanced Plus/ Superior Level would be geared to the development of the ability to support opinion, to convince, negotiate, and to deal with abstract as well as concrete topics (Kaplan and Sinclair, 15). These courses would include experience within all skill areas and would not necessarily be book-oriented. The emphasis would be on transmitting subject matter, not on consciously developing language skills, although the latter would be expected to improve also (Huberman and Medish, 10; Lee, 20).

The foreign language specialist/major

A third suggestion concerns the foreign language specialist or major. In a proficiency-based curriculum, the foreign language specialists or majors would be first and foremost learners who have had an opportunity to build a solid foundation of language skills. In order to ensure and encourage this, the traditional undergraduate foreign language curriculum will have to be enlarged to include learning experiences outside the classroom. Study abroad is, of course, an obvious possibility. Departments should also, however, explore the possibility of setting up immersion experiences for their students in the form of weekends and summer programs, language houses, and so forth.

There is little new here; only the focus has changed. Instead of experiential language study being nice but not absolutely necessary, it would be an integral part of the program for all. Although this may seem idealistic and impractical, the facts as we know them indicate that this is the only means whereby foreign language majors will be able to attain Superior-Level language skills, if indeed that is the proficiency level desired (Muyskens, 24).

Course work should include classes dealing with the language itself (oral vs. written language, dialect variation, stylistics, translation, etc.), as well as courses dealing with culture, civilization, and literature. Although students may choose to specialize primarily in one area, the undergraduate curriculum should ensure that all three areas are included. Further specialization should be restricted to graduate programs.

Obviously, these proposals are sketchy and have implications and ramifications that far exceed the limits of this chapter. Nevertheless, they are put forth here not as absolutes or even as patterns, but as ideas whose validity can only be proven in practice.

Proficiency and the Future

Proficiency, as the organizing principle, represents the first serious attempt at professional unity since the days of NDEA institutes and the comforting security of audiolingualism. The ultimate outcome of this effort remains to be seen. Three possible, but not necessarily mutually exclusive, visions of the future can, however, be imagined.

1994: Vision I

Proficiency, after a few golden years in the late 1980s, has fallen on hard times. Although a large number of teachers were trained in the Oral Proficiency Interview, few returned to participate in followup workshops, and even fewer were interested in any effort at maintaining even local standards, let alone contributing to the establishment of national standards.

The term *Novice* has replaced *Beginner,* but little else has changed. It is not uncommon to find that students rated as Intermediate at one university are found to be Novice or even Advanced at another. Articulation between high schools and colleges has remained in much the sorry state it has always been. Only the names have changed.

Another problem concerns the widening schism between literature teachers and language teachers. This was made worse by the initial tendency to equate proficiency with oral skills plus a tendency for people primarily interested in literature to be excluded from workshops, either through their own lack of interest or through benign neglect on the part of their colleagues. As a result, the already existing gap between language courses and literature courses has widened even more. Unfortunately, both sides have dug in, and in some places, there is even a move afoot for administrators to separate the language courses from the literature courses since objectives and methods in both are impossibly far apart. There are even those who maintain that language courses represent skill courses analogous to golf and tennis and, as such, do not deserve a place in the curriculum at the postsecondary level. A recent survey has verified this, showing that proficiency-based programs are much in evidence at community and junior colleges, somewhat less so at undergraduate institutions, and rarely at primarily research-oriented universities.

At the secondary level, various administrators and teachers saw proficiency testing as the answer to their problems. In some areas, schools began demanding that all classroom teachers have a rating of Superior in speaking before being certified or in order to maintain their certification. Unfortunately, the colleges and universities were not producing many Superior-Level speakers, and the few they did graduate tended to go into business rather than education.

In the case of teachers already in the classroom, the situation was even more disastrous. Many otherwise competent teachers were found to be only at the Advanced Level and some were found to be only Intermediates. Teachers complained that their training had not been proficiency-oriented, and that even if they had at one time managed to acquire what they considered to be "superior" oral-language skills, years of talking "Spanish I" or "Russian II" with little opportunity to travel, had taken its toll. So, since no one really knew what to do, the requirement is quietly being ignored out of existence.

As far as actual high school programs, however, there are still many where success is defined in terms of numbers of Intermediate- and Advanced-Level speakers produced. A national indirect test of speaking ability has been developed, and in many areas this has replaced or supplemented previous tests used for advanced placement or college credit. Since, however, some colleges and universities do not accept this new test as valid, students, teachers, and parents are frequently left at a loss.

Finally, although there have been many valiant efforts to produce proficiency-based materials, the general consensus is that by trying to please everybody, nobody has been satisfied. Textbooks are still pretty much the same, although they all seem to have substituted "Situations" for the old "Topics for Conversation and Composition."

In short, things are chaotic. The confusion has reached the point where professional organizations are establishing committees to investigate the possibility of a curriculum based on reading. No one knows quite what will come of this, but it has to be an improvement over present conditions.

1994: Vision II

Proficiency has taken off! There are now fully developed procedures for evaluating performance in listening, reading, writing, and culture, as well as speaking, plus a centralized authority to oversee it all. Evaluations as provided by this testing agency and its affiliates are now the only generally recognized means of documenting language competency. They are used in teacher certification, in decisions concerning foreign language majors, participation in study abroad programs, and in government and industry.

To cite one example, university departments of foreign languages have replaced the "near native or native fluency" part of their advertising for new faculty members with "ILR Level 4 or above required."

In a sense, the tail has really been wagging the dog, but finally the schools have begun to catch up to the requirements of proficiency. Classrooms are now full of students practicing inviting people to parties, calling up plumbers, and describing everything they did since they got up on a given morning. Some students even report memorizing lists of expressions in order to improve their ability to support opinion, and there is much discussion as to the best way to talk about your plans for the summer.

In fact, getting a good rating has replaced getting good grades, and we're beginning to see a few organizations specializing in "oral test preparation." Indeed, the oral interview itself has been the cause of a great deal of anxiety on the part of candidates, some of whom have been known to seek professional help.

At the secondary level, there has been the widespread adoption of a tracking system. Students who show promise are placed in the "Proficiency Program" where the emphasis is clearly on acquiring a rapid and accurate command of the language. The majority of students, however, are still in the regular course where objectives of global understanding and linguistic appreciation are frequently met by staging mock bullfights, putting on skits, and filling in the blanks on worksheets. There is obviously quite a bit of prestige involved in being in the "Proficiency Program" and teachers as well as students feel it to be a real indication of their superiority.

There are some indications of a backlash. There is talk of communicating effectively as being more than an Advanced or Superior rating, and a few retrograde types are still making noises about the humanities and the values of literary studies, but things seem fairly stable for the moment.

1994: Vision III

The idea of proficiency never really took over the entire country, but many of its effects have been long-lasting. There is now a central agency that can certify speaking proficiency for those who need something in addition to a record of classwork. This agency is also responsible for the training of testers and for maintaining standards and reliability.

The other rating scales were developed further but never became quite as generally accepted as the Oral Proficiency Interview and its scale. Instead, these other scales have served as the basis for curriculum and for the writing of achievement tests, as well as more global proficiency tests. Although not everyone is 100 percent in agreement, there is a feeling of unity. More important, however, is the fact that by making the objectives of foreign language learning more realistic, there are more students in foreign language classrooms. The profession is enjoying general public support.

There is continuing innovation and it is evenly spread across the profession. Since classroom teachers at all levels were involved from early on, they have been staunch supporters and have implemented proficiency-based activities in their classrooms to the extent that they seemed realistic. It is probably fair to say, however, that early instruction at all levels tends to be comprehension-based and that there has been a deemphasis on the learning of grammar for its own sake. Teachers reserve class time for activities that build toward language use, and many exercises that used to go on in the classroom now occur on a one-to-one basis between a student and a computer.

Many schools have become convinced of the value of taking foreign language learning out of the classroom. They have sponsored language-learning experiences in the form of student exchanges, immersion weekends, and ethnic festivals, and, of course, study abroad. It is beginning to be realized that teachers, too, need this type of experience regularly, and ways are being sought to make this both more practical and more efficient.

The exact level of proficiency in the various skill areas necessary for teacher certification or for graduating with a major in foreign languages from a college or university has yet to be definitively determined. Although there is general agreement that the criterion should be somewhere in the Advanced Plus/ Superior range, it is recognized that there are many qualities beyond language proficiency that go into making a successful teacher or even a successful foreign language major. Nevertheless, the level of proficiency in general has been rising, and there is hope that with new programs, foreign language learning in the United States will continue to enjoy the respect it has earned.

Summary

This chapter has dealt with the need for a proficiency-based foreign language curriculum, the premises that would underlie such a curriculum, and the forms that it might possibly take. There is no royal road to success here. Proficiency, even as an organizing principle, is not a magic wand. The potential represented by the concept of proficiency and the possibilities of coordination and articulation it embodies will be our responsibility. In the end, we all help create our own visions of the future.

References, Proficiency in Practice: The Foreign Language Curriculum

1. *ACTFL Provisional Proficiency Guidelines.* Hastings-on-Hudson, NY: American Council on the Teaching of Foreign Languages, 1982.
2. Brendel, Gerd A. "A Model for Mastery Learning in German." *ADFL Bulletin* 15 (September 1983):37–40.

3. Carroll, John B. "Foreign Language Proficiency Levels Attained by Language Majors Near Graduation from College." *Foreign Language Annals* 1 (1967):131–51.
4. Foreign Service Institute. "Expected Levels of Absolute Speaking Proficiency in Languages Taught at the Foreign Service Institute." Roslyn, VA: Foreign Service Institute, 1973.
5. Freedman, Morris. "Should Americans Learn to Speak Foreign Languages?" *Chicago Tribune,* Sunday Ed., 5 February 1984, Sec. 5, p. 4.
6. Gaudiani, Claire L. "Foreign Languages and the Humanistic Tradition: The Relationship to the Coming Decade," pp. 5–7 in Dale L. Lange, ed., *Proceedings of the National Conference on Professional Priorities.* Hastings-on-Hudson, NY: American Council on the Teaching of Foreign Languages, 1981.
7. Goodland, John I. *A Place Called School: Prospects for the Future.* New York: McGraw-Hill, 1984.
8. Higgs, Theodore V., ed. *Teaching for Proficiency, the Organizing Principle.* The ACTFL Foreign Language Education Series, vol. 15. Lincolnwood, IL: National Textbook Co., 1984.
9. _____. "Language Teaching and the Quest for the Holy Grail," pp. 1–9 in Theodore V. Higgs, ed., *Teaching for Proficiency, the Organizing Principle.* The ACTFL Foreign Language Education Series, vol. 15. Lincolnwood, IL: National Textbook Co., 1984.
10. Huberman, Gisele, and Vadim Medish. "Content Courses in Foreign Languages." *ADFL Bulletin* 4 (September 1972):62–64.
11. Hye, Allen E. "Planning for Success: A Synthesis of Existing Foreign Language Teaching Methods." *ADFL Bulletin* 15 (November 1983):57–60.
12. Jakobovits, Leon, and Barbara Gordon. "Language Teaching vs. the Teaching of Talk." *International Journal of Psycholinguistics* 16 (1979):5–22.
13. Jones, Randall L. "Testing: A Vital Connection," pp. 237–65 in June K. Phillips, ed., *The Language Connection: From the Classroom to the World.* The ACTFL Foreign Language Education Series, vol. 9. Lincolnwood, IL: National Textbook Co., 1977.
14. Jorstad, Helen L. "New Approaches to Assessment of Language Learning," pp. 121–40 in Thomas H. Geno, ed., *Our Profession: Present Status and Future Direction.* Northeast Conference on the Teaching of Foreign Languages. Middlebury, VT: The Northeast Conference, 1980.
15. Kaplan, Isabelle M., and Margaret Sinclair. "Oral Proficiency Testing and the Foreign Language Curriculum: Two Experiments in Curricular Design for Conversation Classes." *Foreign Language Annals,* in press.
16. Kramsch, Claire J. *Discourse Analysis and Second Language Teaching.* Language in Education: Theory and Practice, no. 37. Washington, DC: Center for Applied Linguistics, 1981.
17. Lafayette, Robert C. "Differentiation of Language Instruction," pp. 67–87 in Frank M. Grittner, ed., *Learning a Second Language.* Seventy-ninth Yearbook of the National Society for the Study of Education. Chicago: University of Chicago Press, 1980.
18. _____, and Lorraine A. Strasheim. "Foreign Language Curricula and Materials for the Twenty-First Century," pp. 29–34 in Dale L. Lange, ed., *Proceedings of the National Conference on Professional Priorities.* Hastings-on-Hudson, NY: American Council on the Teaching of Foreign Languages, 1981.
19. Lange, Dale L. "Using the Oral Proficiency Interview to Evaluate Proficiency in Secondary School French." Paper presented at the Central States Conference on the Teaching of Foreign Languages, Louisville, KY, April 1982.
20. Lee, Vera. "A New Interdisciplinary Program." *ADFL Bulletin* 15 (September 1983):4–6.

21. Liskin-Gasparro, Judith E. "The ACTFL Proficiency Guidelines: A Historical Perspective," pp. 11–42 in Theodore V. Higgs, ed., *Teaching for Proficiency, the Organizing Principle.* The ACTFL Foreign Language Education Series, vol. 15. Lincolnwood, IL: National Textbook Co., 1984.

22. _____, and Protase E. Woodford. "Proficiency Testing in Second Language Classrooms," pp. 124–31 in Robert G. Mead, ed., *The Foreign Language Teacher: The Lifelong Learner.* Northeast Conference on the Teaching of Foreign Languages. Middlebury, VT: The Northeast Conference, 1982.

23. Lowe, Pardee, Jr. *ILR Handbook on Oral Interview Testing.* Washington, DC: DLI/LS Joint Oral Interview Transfer Project, December 1982, Rev. August 1983.

24. Muyskens, Judith A. "Preservice and Inservice Teacher Training: Focus on Proficiency," pp. 179–200 in Theodore V. Higgs, ed., *Teaching for Proficiency, the Organizing Principle.* The ACTFL Foreign Language Education Series, vol. 15. Lincolnwood, IL: National Textbook Co., 1984.

25. Omaggio, Alice C. "The Proficiency-Oriented Classroom," pp. 43–84 in Theodore V. Higgs, ed., *Teaching for Proficiency, the Organizing Principle.* The ACTFL Foreign Language Education Series, vol. 15. Lincolnwood, IL: National Textbook Co., 1984.

26. Pimsleur, Paul, and Johann F. Struth. "Knowing Your Students in Advance." *Modern Language Journal* 53 (February 1969):85–87.

27. Ryder, Frank G. "Foreign Language Study at the Postsecondary Level," pp. 128–49 in Frank M. Grittner, ed., *Learning a Second Language.* Seventy-ninth Yearbook of the National Society for the Study of Education. Chicago: University of Chicago Press, 1980.

28. Stevick, Earl W. "Curriculum Development at the Foreign Service Institute," pp. 85–112 in Theodore V. Higgs, ed., *Teaching for Proficiency, the Organizing Principle.* The ACTFL Foreign Language Education Series, vol. 15. Lincolnwood, IL: National Textbook Co., 1984.

29. Tanner, Daniel, and Laurel N. Tanner. *Curriculum Development: Theory into Practice,* 2nd ed. New York: Macmillan Publishing Co., 1980.

30. Trim, J. L. M. *Developing a Unit/Credit Scheme of Adult Language Learning,* 2nd ed. New York: Pergamon Press, 1980.

31. Valdman, Albert. "The Incorporation of the Notion of Communicative Competence in the Design of the Introductory Foreign Language Course Syllabus," pp. 18–23 in Dale L. Lange, ed., *Proceedings of the National Conference on Professional Priorities.* Hastings-on-Hudson, NY: American Council on the Teaching of Foreign Languages, 1981.

Materials Development for the Proficiency-Oriented Classroom

Jeannette D. Bragger
The Pennsylvania State University

Introduction

Since the publication of the *ACTFL Provisional Proficiency Guidelines* (1) in 1982, much has been done to disseminate the idea of proficiency-based teaching throughout the profession. With the help of government funding, ACTFL has sponsored numerous familiarization and training workshops. Institutions, both secondary and postsecondary, have allocated funds to train their teachers in the administration and rating of the Oral Proficiency Interview. Conference sessions have explored the many implications of the proficiency-based curriculum, and the pedagogical literature has begun to reflect a growing awareness on the part of foreign language educators that proficiency goals in the various skills should be at the heart of foreign language programs. Indeed, significant changes are already evident in the area of textbook publication, as authors and editors begin to reorient materials in accordance with the proficiency guidelines.

Such widespread interest in proficiency has naturally raised many questions about curriculum, course design, course content, and about materials appropriate for use in the proficiency-oriented classroom. This last question is a crucial one since it is clearly not enough to establish program objectives and priorities without also determining what is actually to be done in the classroom and what types of materials are best suited for the

Jeannette D. Bragger (Ph.D., University of California, Santa Barbara) is Associate Professor of French at The Pennsylvania State University, University Park, where she directs the Summer Intensive Language Institute, teaches pedagogy and French civilization, coordinates elementary and postintermediate language courses, and supervises teaching assistants. She is the author of three college French texts, and her publications have appeared in various professional journals. She is a member of ACTFL, AATF, MLA, and has served on the Executive Council of PSMLA. She has served as consultant to the ACTFL/ETS Proficiency Projects and is a trainer in oral proficiency testing.

development of proficiency in the various skills. We will deal with this and related concerns in this chapter.

While pedagogical materials always need to be tailored to the personality of the instructor and to the collective personality of a given group of learners, specific organizing principles also need to be followed if we are to be successful in developing foreign language proficiency. Face and content validity in tests are intrinsically linked to face and content validity in courses. It is therefore important for us to examine textbooks, to influence future directions of published texts, and to introduce the types of materials in and out of the classroom that will neither negate nor conflict with the established goals of a proficiency-oriented program.

The ACTFL Provisional Proficiency Guidelines ⎯⎯⎯⎯⎯

The original oral proficiency descriptions compiled by agencies of the U.S. government (Liskin-Gasparro, 8) were based on observations of native and nonnative speakers of a language in real settings in which they were functioning. The basic orientation, then, was toward natural language use on the job rather than abstract theory. When they were adapted for academic use as the ACTFL guidelines, the rating descriptions respected this orientation. The three criteria for language use in the context of this observable reality are *function, context/content,* and *accuracy,* what is known as the Functional Trisection. The descriptions of each proficiency level include statements about each of these three areas. *Function* refers to the task that an individual is able to accomplish linguistically (asking questions, giving information, describing, narrating, stating and supporting opinion, etc.); *context* or *content* describes the setting in which these functions are carried out; *accuracy* refers to the degree of correctness (grammar, pronunciation, intonation, syntax, etc.) with which the message is delivered. The real language ability of an individual is assessed on the basis of these three factors, with each factor increasing in scope as one moves up the proficiency scale. A corollary is that the assessment is global, that is, based on a holistic view of the speech or writing act. It is with these three principles in mind—the total language act in real situations with regard to function, context, and accuracy—that we must evaluate and create appropriate materials for the language class. Furthermore, materials can be considered appropriate only if their use leads to the development of assessable proficiency.

Prerequisites for Material Creation and Use ⎯⎯⎯⎯⎯

As we prepare to reevaluate teaching materials, we must first reassess our own attitudes. We may, in fact, need to acquire a number of new skills that will enable us to move more effectively toward teaching for proficiency. The guidelines, and particularly the Oral Proficiency Interview (OPI) procedures, can be very useful in restructuring not only teacher attitudes but also student thinking.

The first area of consideration is that of error tolerance versus error correction. All teachers know how to correct, and most of us have probably developed the habit of correcting student speech systematically. The greatest fear many teachers have is that the absence of immediate correction will develop incorrect patterns of speech, which will be impossible to change at a later stage. With the obvious stress on accuracy stated in the guidelines, error correction from the earliest stages is clearly a must if students are to develop good habits. However, there should also be a time when students are allowed to use the language creatively without constant intervention from the "expert." When is it appropriate to correct in order to prevent the acquisition of bad habits, and when should we refrain from correction in order to allow the development of creative language use? To phrase the question more precisely, when should correction be immediate and when should it be delayed?

If we accept the concepts of skill-getting and skill-using advanced by Rivers (12, 13), we arrive at a partial answer to this question. Ideally, each class period should contain elements of both skill-getting and skill-using. If we organize lesson plans according to these two principles, we can also decide ahead of time which exercises and activities are designed to give students the skills they need to communicate (grammar explanations, pronunciation drills, controlled structural exercises, vocabulary study, simulated communication, etc.). During this phase, systematic correction (done positively) is clearly in order. During follow-up work (skill-using), which includes communicative activities, small group work, games, role playing, and simulations, is the time when students should be given the chance to "try their wings" and enter into meaningful communication with their classmates or instructor. It is also the time when, while listening to their speech production, the teacher is advised to keep his or her distance and to note errors for correction at a later point. Delayed correction can occur after the activity has been completed or in a subsequent lesson. Intervention should occur only if misunderstanding is preventing students from accomplishing their assigned tasks.

Skill-getting and skill-using should not, however, be seen as a set of separate and distinct activities. In fact, Rivers (12) warns against just such a dichotomy. "Skill-using activities . . . should spring naturally and inevitably from the types of activities engaged in for skill-getting" (p. 56). Although, as teachers, we are well aware of the division and will even plan for it, smooth transitions from one to the other should give students a sense of coherence and cohesion. How we plan our daily lessons is crucial to the outcome and cannot be overestimated in the development of foreign language proficiency.

Modification of Teacher Behaviors

The Oral Proficiency Interview procedures contain many basic rules that may help teachers modify some of their classroom behaviors. In the interview, the interviewer is instructed not to interrupt students when they are speaking, to refrain from correcting; to refrain from supplying information, missing words, and correct grammar forms; to refrain from filling the silences that occur because students are thinking about what they wish to say. In other words, while meaningful communication is going on, such communication must be able to proceed unimpeded, and the flow of ideas must not be interrupted. During the interview, students demonstrate their ability to cope linguistically without the traditional teacher aids normally supplied in the classroom. They are working with an interviewer who is patient, who responds in a natural way to what they say, who may offer encouragement through facial expressions but does not put words in their mouths or dominate the conversation. Teachers who have become interviewers often comment on the influence that interview behaviors have had on them in their dealings with students in the class-room. In particular, they have noted an increased willingness to restrain the impulse to intervene, and although they may still cringe inwardly at the errors they hear, they have observed a marked decrease in student fears and inhibitions.

As has been stated earlier, this is not to suggest that we ignore errors, but rather that we find a time more appropriate for their correction than in the middle of a conversation. Delayed correction has the additional advantage of being addressed to the entire class rather than to a particular student. The most important result of this type of behavior modification on the part of the teacher is that it gives students the kind of freedom they would experience when actually speaking the language in the target culture. This freedom will keep them from becoming too dependent on the teacher and will teach them that they have available many of their own resources, that they may know much more than they suspected, and that they can trust themselves to function when they are called upon to do so. Once established, such self-confidence will inevitably spill over into the rest of their language learning.

Another behavioral adjustment that teachers are advised to make is in the type of language they use with their students in class. Typical "teacher talk," replete with statements such as "very good," "très bien," or "sehr gut," evaluates language rather than showing interest in ideas; it tends to be artificial and is not likely to be encountered by students in conversations with people in real situations. What kind of language role model should the teacher be? The following considerations may be helpful in evaluating ourselves as language models.

1. *Rate of speech.* Are we consistently slowing down in an exaggerated manner, giving students the impression that this is the way in which the language is spoken in the target culture? When is a slower rate of speech appropriate and when is it not? Perhaps the decision can once again be made according to the principles of skill-getting and skill-using. When we are teaching, i.e., appealing explicitly to the analytical side of student behavior, we may slow down to be sure that students grasp what we want them to learn. When we are *communicating* with them, however, a normal rate of speech should be the norm. After all, our goal is not to teach a version of the foreign language that can be used only between student and teacher but rather between a student and any native speaker of the language.

2. *Level of language.* Particularly at beginning levels, a common tendency is to oversimplify; to avoid colloquial speech, as well as structures and vocabulary that have not been taught; to restrict verb forms to the present tense; to use what some have called baby talk. In fact, this again represents "teacher talk," a result of our concern about helping students that may ultimately hinder them in the real world. Although they may not be ready to use a higher level of language, the more exposure they have to it, the more likely they will be able to understand what is happening when they are put into the real setting of the target culture. This is not to suggest that we move so far beyond their language abilities that communication breaks down, but it is to suggest that even if they have not explicitly learned to use the past tense, for example, we also must refrain from using it.

3. *Remodeling.* The procedure we have all developed of giving back answers in a more polished and grammatically correct form may be appropriate during the learning phase, when we are trying to instill accurate use of structures and vocabulary. However, it should be used in conversations only when it is natural to do so. In "real" speech, we use remodeling not to express approval or disapproval of the linguistic patterns used by the speaker but rather to emphasize or express surprise, disagreement, or another form of commentary on the message that is being transmitted. For example: "Yesterday, I finally told him what I thought about his idea!" Remodeling to show surprise might consist of the following response: "You *actually* told him what you thought of his idea?" First, the word *actually* adds emphasis to the idea of surprise. Second, the repetition of the exact words confirms the feeling of surprise. What the remodeling does not do, however, is comment on the grammar, syntax, or vocabulary used by the speaker. For the teacher, avoidance of the remodeling habit might also indicate a greater confidence in the student to communicate. It is the recognition, at the right time, that communication took place, that the student was successful, that he or she understood the message. Positive reinforcement is much more important in the long run than the distressing

attitude that correctness *always* takes precedence over the content of the message. The risk we run in failing to acknowledge real communication when it takes place is that students begin to feel that it does not really matter what they say as long as they say it correctly. The result will probably be neutral speech, devoid of real personal meaning, devoid of personal commitment to the message, the reluctance to say anything meaningful because "I don't know how to say what I want to say, so I'll opt for what is simple and correct."

4. *Complete sentences.* Teacher insistence that students always respond in complete sentences may add to the artificiality of the language produced in the classroom. Once again, complete sentences may be appropriate when students are just beginning to learn a new structure, when they are in the process of skill-getting. However, if we analyze everyday speech, we find that all of us readily use sentence fragments, we do not always repeat the if-clause of a conditional sentence, and we often respond in short utterances. No one is shocked when this occurs in one's native language, but few of us seem to have the same tolerance in the language classroom.

Much of the behavior that has been discussed in the preceding paragraphs is the result of our fear that the student's experience with the foreign language will somehow be incomplete or inadequate if we do not systematically correct, remodel, and so forth. However, we may in fact be teaching students to be unwilling to take a chance, to refuse to speak up unless they have formulated the correct sentences in their minds ahead of the speech act. The spontaneity and improvisation necessary to real communication can be stifled at the outset and can leave students handicapped in ways that we never imagined or intended.

The obvious conclusion to be drawn is that we, as teachers, need to increase our tolerance for error without, at the same time, losing our concern for accuracy. Perhaps the only way we will accomplish this is to decide when error tolerance is appropriate and when systematic correction is in order. A concurrent benefit may be that we will teach students to be willing to be creative, to try out what they have learned, to explore new word combinations, and to be willing to respond honestly rather than with standard, memorized phrases. The same principles apply to writing skills, where we often reward those students who try nothing new but keep to what they know to be absolutely correct, leaving their concern for real communication inhibited or stilled altogether.

A close reading of the guidelines can help us to determine where error tolerance is appropriate, which errors we should be willing to accept at which level, and which structures and vocabulary should no longer be subject to error. It is clear that the Novice speaker will make many errors in the few verb conjugations and tenses he or she has learned. At this level, where we might not be tolerant of errors in certain lexical items or memorized phrases, our patience should be greater for other elements which we know are going to stabilize at a later stage in language acquisition. At the Intermediate Level, we should become less and less tolerant of student inability to ask questions correctly or to accurately use the present tense of the most high-frequency verbs. Our tolerance of tense error may, however, still be fairly high at this level. Accuracy in verb tenses becomes imperative once we move to the Advanced Level. Although errors are still to be expected, the commonly used verbs and tenses are presumed to be controlled. However, conditional sentences may only just be emerging, so we will want to give them a chance to develop more fully before we become exigent. Immediate and delayed correction in the skill-getting and skill-using phases will eventually increase language accuracy while at the same time encouraging students to convey personally authentic messages.

The nature and ground rules of the Oral Proficiency Interview permit students to express themselves without interference or help from the interviewer. Experience has shown that many students are surprised at their ability to converse with someone for ten to twenty minutes and that they are able to do so without teacher prompting. They are surprised at what they know, what they can say and do with language, how relatively easy it is to have a "real" conversation. The interviewer is the one who knows how "real" the conversation was, but regardless of this judgment, the student is left with a positive feeling. Perhaps this is what students should be helped to feel at the end of the class period. Rather than leaving the class with the echo of everything they did wrong, they will remember what they did well, and perhaps they will gain the confidence to be creative, to make the best use of whatever "chunks" of language they know, and to be willing to venture into unknown territory. They will have *learned* what they need to improve, they will *know* what they can already do well.

Materials Development and Use

Once we fully accept and put into practice the idea that everything we do with the language must be authentic, we are in a better position to create the appropriate materials that will attain our stated objectives.

The idea of materials development immediately raises protestations of insufficient available time. Whether we teach at the secondary or post-secondary levels, all of us, for different reasons, suffer from time constraints that may keep us from acting on the many ideas we have. Therefore, the first priority should be to examine materials already available to us, materials we have already acquired that we can modify without undue additional work.

Although the most obvious source of class content and ideas is the textbook itself, using it as a tool to be adapted to the individual's style of teaching rather than as a prescriptive set of inflexible rules is a basic step in the movement toward a proficiency-oriented classroom.

Unfortunately, the greater part of our language curriculum and the lesson plan is still tied to the book and grammatical ordering rather than structured according to functions or task universals. Much has been said and written to discourage such textbook dependency, yet little has in fact been done to change it. Hammerly (5, p. 201), recognizing the problem, suggests that more harm than good comes from reliance on textbooks:

> One of the most harmful factors in a second language program is excessive reliance on textbooks. Textbooks, unfortunately, tend to dominate second language teaching. They are always there, setting an unreasonably fast pace, always open, interfering with the development of the audiolingual skills and reinforcing the wrong notion that *the* language is what is found in books. The belief that a second language can be learned from textbooks is most damaging to second language learning and needs to be eliminated. Much would be gained by banning textbooks from the second language classroom, reducing them to homework and laboratory workshops subordinated to cassette tape recordings.

What this seemingly extreme position suggests is that teacher attitudes toward textbooks must be changed and that the place of texts in the learning process needs to be reevaluated.

A brief synopsis of how most textbooks come into being may be helpful in placing their use into the right perspective. Most authors decide to write a textbook because they have seen serious inadequacies in the books they have used themselves. Whether these inadequacies are real or perceived is, of course, open to debate. Nevertheless, authors have an idea of how something that is already on the market could be improved, they present a prospectus and sample chapters to various publishers, and if their ideas seem to be sufficiently original, they succeed in getting a contract. At the outset, authors may be very optimistic and even idealistic about the extent of their anticipated accomplishments. As they begin the task of writing, however, they discover that if anyone is ever going to see the book, if it is to be completed, if it is going to be used in the classroom, many compromises will have to be made. Acting in good faith, both publishers and authors are concerned not only with the pedagogical soundness of their text but also with the remuneration to be obtained from its adoptions. They hope their work will be recognized as meritorious and will therefore reward them tangibly for the many months or years they have spent on its preparation. Those who are most influential in effecting compromises and modifications in manuscripts are the reviewers, i.e., the teachers who have been called upon to comment on the work as it is being produced. This is where teachers in the profession can exercise a great deal of influence, but this is precisely the area in which they often choose to exercise it the least. Many teachers, although they may have very good ideas about how texts might be changed, never bother to convey these ideas to the publisher or the authors. Those teachers who are reviewers know how much influence they can exert on the form the final product will have when the text is published. But a high percentage of teachers adheres to a policy of noninvolvement, which may have the following consequences: (1) many good ideas do not find their way into textbooks; (2) textbook reviewing is done by a select few who, no matter how competent, cannot accurately reflect the viewpoints and ideas of everyone in the profession; (3) this minority, working with authors and publishers, determines the types of texts that are likely to appear on the market; (4) although every effort is made to obtain representative reviews, it is possible that this minority may, at times, be either somewhat conservative or perhaps too liberal, or one that is particularly obsessed by some of the fears discussed previously.

It is not our intention to belittle contributions made by many of the excellent manuscript reviewers who do their work conscientiously and who are informed about the latest developments in language pedagogy. The point is that the sampling may be too small, that it may be prejudiced in one direction or another, and that many good ideas can be lost because not enough different people are involved in the process. Both publishers and authors are very sensitive to the demands of the market, and they seek as much feedback as possible. They may reject some ideas and accept others, but they must obtain the approval of as many teachers as possible in order to sell the book and to disseminate the pedagogical principles that they espouse and find to be valid.

Who is really "responsible" for the final product, the textbook that finally appears on the market? The publishers and authors, of course, but perhaps more important the people in the teaching profession who have expressed their needs and ideas. Too often, this aspect of textbook production is overlooked, and the result is criticism of publishers and particularly of authors. Reluctance to use the influence we all possess with respect to published materials may result in texts that are not particularly suited to our needs. However, every textbook must be looked upon as a flexible tool designed to help us, not restrict us, in our teaching. We, therefore, need to examine a text very carefully before deciding whether or not it is appropriate and, more important, whether it can be sufficiently modified to fit the objectives set forth in the guidelines.

What are the essential components in the development of proficiency, and what indications can we get from a textbook that it indeed includes these components? One must remember that a textbook is a commercial venture and that much will be done in order to enhance the sales figures. Claims made in publicity materials should be verified by teachers through a close reading of the preface *and* the text itself. In some cases, claims may be justified to a certain degree, but it is also possible that they are greatly exaggerated.

With the rapid spread of proficiency, the claim most commonly made is that a textbook or program will lead to a specified level of proficiency. This point is worth examination since it should be remembered that textbooks themselves *do not* lead to proficiency. The development of proficiency in any skill area can only be accomplished by the teacher through a judicious choice of materials that will support, not contradict, what is being done in the class.

Assessment of textbooks

Having examined the claims made by authors and publishers, one should be careful to peruse each component of the textbook. Just as a publisher must evaluate the complete manuscript before giving an author a contract, teachers must take the time to examine the entire book carefully before making a choice. What should be considered to determine whether the text in question supports the idea of proficiency development and accurate communication of messages? The following guidelines may be useful in making a fair assessment of any text and in modifying it as necessary.

Vocabulary. Are all of the vocabulary groups (foods, etc.) limited to a list of generic terms, or do they include possibilities for students to express their *real* preferences? Must students say that they like ham and that they eat it often even if they do not? Are they given real choices or are differences of personality and taste not taken into account? This is a task that falls once again on the teacher who must be aware of the desire in every individual to express personal preference. When asked for information by a student, responses such as "We will get to this later" or "You'll find this out in the next chapter" or "Let's not worry about food right now, we'll get to it next week" suggest that knowledge can be compartmentalized and that our minds function the way chapters are organized in a book.

How useful is generic vocabulary in real life? Can students really go into a restaurant in France, Germany, or Spain and order "meat"? It is clear that any one book cannot reflect the preferences of all the students who may use the text. However, it is possible for the book to include activities and exercises that require students to find out how to talk about their real preferences. They may do this simply by asking the instructor, using a dictionary, or asking other students. If such exercises do not exist, it is up to the teacher to add them. It is important that students be given sufficient vocabulary to really be able to order a meal and to really get what they ordered. However, a commonly voiced complaint is that authors present too much vocabulary in their attempt to account for individual differences. To achieve a better balance agreeable to everyone, it would perhaps be advisable to start thinking, from the beginning of language study, in terms of personal vocabulary lists. Students can be asked to keep a notebook in which they write lexical items and expressions that they want to learn and use, words and expressions that have personal meaning for them. In addition to listing these items, students may be asked to use the words in at least two contexts. Once they have written their sentences or short paragraphs, they can be asked to record these on a cassette tape. Both the notebooks and the cassettes will be checked periodically by the teacher. The notebooks may also include a special section in which students list English words they want to have translated by the teacher. Apart from the personalized list, students will, of course, be held responsible for a core group of vocabulary items common to everyone in the class. To ensure that real use will be made of both categories of items, teachers should include both in their oral and written tests.

Another consideration when looking at vocabulary is whether it is current and of high frequency and whether it includes functional items that are applicable to many contexts. Other than grammatical constructions, much of what is first acquired by students is memorized as lexical items. Students may not necessarily know how to generalize grammatically on the expression or they may not know how to conjugate a verb in the conditional tense, but they may have learned to use a set of expressions (such as polite requests) that allows them to communicate without having the ability to analyze. This is particularly true of idiomatic expressions, conversational fillers, ways of agreeing and disagreeing, and so forth. When students list words and expressions they would like to learn in their personal vocabulary notebooks, they are defining what is high frequency to them. Because most teachers and authors are no longer teenagers or may not have teenagers in the home, instructors will not always know what, in lexical terms, is of most immediate importance to their students. For example, teachers may know that Michael Jackson is at the top of the charts, but what vocabulary do students use to express their liking for the singer?

Another consideration when studying an author's use of vocabulary is the extent to which it allows students to express feelings. Is everything limited to statements without the possibility of commentary? If expression of feelings is possible, does it exist only in extremes—love or hate, always or never—or are shades and nuances possible?

Does the initial exposure to a new vocabulary group reflect the immediate interests and concerns of American students, allowing them to deal with their own environment, or does it lead them immediately into the unknown spheres of the target culture? Since we know that most people prefer to talk about themselves before looking at others, we must capitalize on this egocentric attitude. For example, when dealing with education and studies, does the text first teach students to describe their own experiences in school, their own course work and school system, leading them secondly to the description of the educational system in the target culture, or is it the reverse? We strongly support the argument that a language learner is more likely to remember vocabulary and structures if they are of immediate relevance. In the long run, students will be able to cope better with the foreign environment if they have first defined their own.

Finally, is vocabulary ordered to move from the concrete to the abstract? The proficiency descriptions clearly indicate that Novice and Intermediate speakers are most comfortable with concrete reality; the abstract does not become a major factor until the Advanced and Superior levels. Because abstractions are more difficult to deal with even in one's native language, it is reasonable to assume that they will develop at a later stage in the language acquisition process.

Grammar sequencing and explanations. Given what Novice- and Intermediate-Level speakers will need in order to function more or less effectively in the language, it is important to consider the question of grammar sequencing and explanations in textbooks. First-year texts that delay use of the past tense until the latter part of the book can be extremely limiting. Although control of the past tenses is not expected until the Advanced Level, it is difficult to create with the language when one is limited to the present tense. Equally annoying are explanations that are so in-depth that they create unnecessary complications, hindering rather than helping students in their attempts to communicate.

Does the textbook treat students as intelligent people or does it patronize them and make assumptions that students cannot handle a given topic, that they are all intellectually underdeveloped, that they cannot handle the unexpected? In other words, is the text intelligently done, presenting challenges while at the same time assuming that students are capable of meeting the challenges? Underestimation of students either by the authors or by the instructors is a self-fulfilling prophecy. If we believe students *cannot* do it, it is very likely that they *will not* do it. Establishing the proper, positive environment will not solve all of our problems. But real learning is more likely to take place in a positive environment.

Exercise types and activities. Do exercises lead to real communication or does the book stop short of skill-using? Are exercises contextualized simply to give us the illusion of reality, or are they in fact contextualized? Is there a chance for students to become acquainted with new structures through some simple transformation exercises that have no need to be disguised as anything else? Are these drills followed by cognitive exercises to reinforce structures? Are the cognitive exercises contextualized and personalized? If they are not, is it easy enough for teachers to transform them to give them more meaning and relevance? One of the most typical problems in exercises is that they are composed of a series of non sequiturs, unrelated statements that not only demand manipulation of the language but also require considerable mental acrobatics.

Perhaps one of the reasons why students do not answer our questions or follow along easily in exercises is that we are asking them to do something that is simply not a normal process for the human mind. Consider the following exchange, for example, taken from an Oral Proficiency Interview. The sample is translated from the French.

Question: Where did you spend your last vacation, Paul?
Answer: In California.
Question: What did you do in California?
Answer: I went to Disneyland and I went to the beach.
Question: What is your sister like?
[The question had to be repeated twice before Paul answered it.]

The first part of this exchange is a very natural one because there is follow-up in the same context. The last question, however, led to a breakdown in communication because Paul was still thinking about his vacation in California. Since his sister was not with him on this trip (we found this out later), she was not uppermost in his mind and it took him considerable time to reorient his thinking. Furthermore, we discovered that Paul had no difficulty talking about his sister. His hesitation was not due to inadequacies in his language but rather to the required mental readjustment when the context was changed too abruptly.

The Oral Proficiency Interview, simulating a real conversation, teaches us to avoid this type of disconnected discourse and to change contexts more naturally as we would in real conversations. The technique to accomplish this can be applied easily to textbook exercises. A grammar transformation drill containing ten unrelated items (sentences, questions, etc.) can be transformed to allow follow-up on a particular topic. In many instances it suffices to establish the theme in the directions and to define the characters participating in the activities presented in the exercise. For example, instead of giving ten sentences to be put into the past tense, the directions could read:

The Dupont family is sitting around the dinner table discussing the activities of the day. As each member of the family is being questioned, supply the answers using the elements in parentheses.

Model: What did you do today, Susan? (to have / very bad day)
           I had a very bad day.

1. What happened? (to lock / keys in the car)
   (I locked my keys in the car.)
2. What did you do? (to come home / to get the spare keys)
   (I came home and got the spare keys.)

The questioning of Susan can continue if one wishes before focusing on another member of the family. It should be noted that the model question does not elicit the typical exercise answer, but rather a natural conversational answer. This helps impress upon students that questions often lead to unexpected answers that are nevertheless understood in context by both conversational partners. For example, the question "What time is it?" will not necessarily lead to "It's three o'clock." The answer could just as easily be "Oh, my goodness, it's late, I've got to run!"

Real language use. The next important thing to look for in a text is whether or not real language use follows transformational exercises. Activities should involve simulations demanding the transmittal of information in a meaningful context. In the past, textbooks have unfortunately stopped before this most essential step in proficiency development. Do the activities require students to simply describe the situation or do they in fact make them carry out a specific task linguistically? For example, is the activity limited to describing what has to be done if one wants to send a package airmail from Paris to New York, or is the student required to role-play the situation with the teacher or another student playing the part of the post office employee? Too often, when we are short of time, this is precisely what we leave out of the classroom because we feel that it is more important to "cover" the material as presented in the textbook and to prepare students for the discrete-point achievement exams typical of most courses. If the textbook does not contain any such activities, as many now do, it is relatively simple for the teacher to invent them. The model for situations is again supplied by the Oral Proficiency Interview. At every proficiency level except Novice and ILR Levels 4 and 5, the interviewee is asked to get into, through, and out of a situation described in his or her native language on a situation card. For American students, this card will be in English. The reason for this is that we do not wish to give away either the vocabulary or the structures necessary to successfully accomplish the assigned task. The following are two situations from a first-year French textbook. The first situation is appropriate for the Intermediate Level, the second for the Advanced Level.

You would like a friend to go to the movies with you.

1. Find out when he/she is free.
2. Invite him/her to go to a movie.
3. Discuss the kind of movie you would like to see.
4. Arrange a time and meeting place.
5. Decide whether you will do anything else that evening.
[Bragger and Rice, 2, p. 523.]

You and a friend are staying in a small hotel in Paris. Around midnight your friend complains of being sick (cramps, chills, fever). You go to the desk in the lobby and ask for help.

1. Explain the problem to the desk clerk.
2. Ask if there is a drugstore in the neighborhood that stays open late at night.
3. Ask for directions on how to get there; repeat the directions to verify that you have heard them correctly.
4. Go to the drugstore and explain your friend's problem to the druggist.
5. Ask for some medicine.
6. Find out if there are special instructions as to how the medicine should be taken.
[Bragger and Rice, 2, p. 524.]

In creating these situations, care should be taken to control the vocabulary and structures in such a way that the student cannot simply translate from the English. It may also be preferable for the instructor to play the role of the target language official or professional if the situation calls for one. It is not likely that any of our students will ever be druggists or hotel clerks in the target culture.

Photographs and illustrations. Are photographs and illustrations in the textbook *only* included for artistic reasons, or are students asked to work with them, analyze them, or use them to further their cultural understanding? Too often, photographs are impossible to describe even in one's native language, particularly if they are limited to nature and architectural themes and do not include people engaged in specific and identifiable activities. A photo of the front portal of a French chateau will not lead to a great deal of discussion if the student is still limited to concrete terminology and has not yet learned to fantasize with the language in order to see beyond the portal. And, if the student says that the photo represents a *porte* (door), this will in any case not be accurate architecturally. It is important for teachers to analyze the photographs, to see how well they fit in with what is being learned in a particular chapter and how much their content offers possibilities for discussion and/or role-play.

One simple way to integrate photos into the class activities is to make slides of the best ones and to discuss these as a group. Another suggestion would be for the teacher to make up activities surrounding the photo content. Questions might include: "What do you think people are saying to each other in this photo?" "Act out the conversation that you think is taking place between the two friends in the café." "What do you see in this open-air market scene that you would not see in a market in the United States?" "Describe the clothing the people in the photo are wearing."

"What is unusual about their clothing?" Some questions require students to use imagination. If a photo represents business people in an office, they can be asked to talk about where each one got his or her education, where they grew up, what their family background is, how much money they make, whether or not they are married and have children, etc. It is clear that many types of activities can succeed only if students are willing to be inventive. The photo, of course, cannot really tell us the nature of the conversation between the shopper and the checker in a supermarket, but it will serve as a springboard for communication in a real setting.

Chapter or unit objectives. Do the various chapters or units of a textbook, either explicitly or implicitly, indicate the objectives in terms of function, context/content, and accuracy? Is it clear what tasks students should be able to carry out linguistically when they have finished a given segment? Or is there a vague promise of teaching the four skills, each of them developed without direction or specific objectives? If objectives do not exist, it behooves the teacher to establish them for each segment. Once these objectives have been established, it will be much easier to develop a functional syllabus, explicitly stating to students what tasks they will learn to accomplish.

Proficiency Guidelines and the Lesson Plan

It is not enough to have a coherent proficiency-oriented curriculum. It is equally if not more important to follow through on the stated curricular objectives and to plan each class period carefully so that class content contributes to the overall furthering of proficiency goals. Each lesson plan should be a detailed version of the syllabus entry for the day, and each segment of the lesson plan should be included for very specific reasons that are meant to constitute one element in the picture as a whole.

This, in combination with the textbook materials, may mean a certain reordering of the sequence of presentation in the textbook itself. The larger questions that have to be asked first are: What do I want my students to be able to do well at the end of today's class? What do I want to have introduced to them? If there is an interweaving of learning activities (skill-getting) and acquisition activities (skill-using), students can perfect one task while entering into a new one. If we need objectives for curriculum and individual periods, we should also be clear about our objectives for each activity in which we choose to have students participate. What aspect of the larger context is enhanced by this vocabulary group? How does this structure help students to expand the context, and am I making them aware of this? Are students aware of the most frequent contexts in which this structure is likely to appear and have they had ample time to work in this context? If the instructor keeps in mind the larger picture and objective and helps students make the association between seemingly (to the student) disconnected chunks of language, the successful development of proficiency is more likely to occur.

Is there a time during the class period when students can get information from the teacher about something they want to know how to say? Is there a good balance between structured and open-ended activities? When should correction occur systematically, and when should it be delayed? Have students had the chance to create with the language? Does this game have a real linguistic base or is it a game for its own sake? Are students integrating the various skills (speaking, listening, reading, writing)? Are the exercises contextualized and personalized? Is every activity totally predictable, or are there some that require students to be creative and to use circumlocution? Are there enough contexts so that a variety of language factors can be demonstrated?

These and other questions should be asked during the preparation of the lesson plan. Although the plan should always be flexible to accommodate spur-of-the-moment change, there should be enough structure to guide both instructor and students. Before-class preparation is therefore crucial to a well-organized and well-run class and is the means by which we can continue building toward proficiency. However, reevaluation of the plan after the class is finished may be equally important. Now that ideas have been put into practice, it is time to decide whether they indeed fulfilled expectations and accomplished what they were meant to accomplish. It is during this after-the-fact phase that we can make some modifications, noting what worked well and what did not. In short, what we end up with is an annotated lesson plan based on experience that will be all the more useful the next time the class is taught. Constant revision of the various elements and constant addition of new activities assure a pace and variety interesting not only to the students but also to the instructor.

Materials Appropriate for Various Proficiency Levels ____

When we say that we are teaching four-skills courses, what do we really mean and what do we do to develop these skills systematically? How do we integrate culture? What are our expectations in a French I, German I, or Spanish I course, and what materials are appropriate to maximize learning at that particular level?

The ACTFL Proficiency Guidelines themselves may be the best indicators of appropriate materials. For each skill, the statements of function, context/content, and accuracy help us to determine at what level students are operating, what grammar structures they should be working with, which contexts they are most comfortable with, and what tasks, if any, they need to be able to accomplish successfully. The descriptions also indicate which aspects of each of the skills contribute most to the successful completion of the task at the various levels. For example, at a particular proficiency level, vocabulary may play the most important part in any communication that will take place. At another level, grammar (accuracy) begins to peak and correctness has precedence over other aspects. Fluency in speaking will enter at a higher level, and any sociolinguistic features demonstrating both understanding of cultural patterns and their assimilation will be more prominent at even higher levels. The inherent assumption is that a student's speaking, listening, reading or writing, and culture are being compared to those of the Educated Native Speaker, whose elements of language are all equally developed if not always equally used at any one time.

In the following pages, we will suggest materials associated with the various levels of proficiency, as well as some of their uses in the classroom. It is often difficult to distinguish between the materials and the techniques needed to use them effectively. The best materials will not help to develop proficiency if instructors do not treat them with proficiency in mind. They will simply become additional texts, realia, songs, etc. to be included in an already large collection of similar materials.

For the sake of continuity, we will present suggestions for materials development with abbreviated proficiency descriptions from Novice to Superior. Rather than assume that each level necessitates an entirely new set of materials and techniques, we should be aware of the basic principle put forth in the Oral Proficiency Interview, i.e., all materials, all contexts can be upgraded to fit the level at which we are working.

To illustrate this principle, let us look at a typical advertisement for a car. The ad probably shows a sleek machine, in an appealing color, with a large trunk in which a family is packing belongings in order to leave for vacation. To show the roominess of the trunk, each member of the family is putting a variety of things into the car. At the Novice Level, students simply enumerate what they see in the ad. As their skills improve, they will add verbs to explain what the family members are doing. Moving to an even higher level (Advanced or Superior), students can be asked to explain why they think each person has chosen to pack a particular object. They can conjecture on where the family is going according to the objects being packed. They can talk about the car and its features. Upgrading even further, students can discuss the role cars play in our society as status symbols, the problems they create (pollution, accidents, etc.); they can move to the rules of the road and compare European rules to those in America. Students can then talk about the car industry, the ups and downs of the American car companies, the competition from France, Germany, and particularly Japan. The possibilities are endless. This example illustrates that one simple picture from a magazine has many potential uses and cuts down on the work we have to do for the various classes we teach, from beginning to advanced. The same ad can then, of course, be utilized for skills other than speaking: students can write about any of the topics they have discussed; they can listen to a taped conversation of two people debating what type of car to buy and the pros and cons of the new models; they can listen to a salesperson convincing someone to buy a particular car; they can participate in situations at the gas station, a car breakdown on the road, telephoning the garage, asking for specific services, and so forth.

One of the main principles of the Oral Proficiency Interview is that no one context is reserved for one proficiency level. Each context is upgraded and made more complicated and abstract as the interviewer encourages and judges the interviewee. It is evident that materials upgrading will also greatly simplify the task of instructors when they collect or create materials for the classroom.

As one may have assumed from the preceding pages, all the examples for materials and activities are given in English. The proficiency guidelines summarized here come from the generic descriptions and may therefore be applied to any language. (See Appendix A.)

Progression of functions from Novice to Superior levels. Novice-Level speakers have practically no functional ability, although they can communicate very simply with memorized material. At the Intermediate Level, they can get into, through, and out of simple survival situations; ask questions; answer questions; and create with the language. At the Advanced Level, they can get into, through, and out of survival situations with a complication; narrate and describe in present, past, and future time. At the Superior Level, they can handle unfamiliar topics or situations, hypothesize, and provide supported opinion.

Context/content from Novice to Superior levels. Novice-Level speakers are able to operate within limited concrete subject areas—basic objects, colors, clothing, family members, weather, weekdays, months, the day's date, and time. At the Intermediate Level, they can handle simple question-and-answer situations, familiar topics within the scope of very limited language experience, routine travel needs, minimum courtesy requirements, everyday survival topics. At the Advanced Level, they are able to discuss recreational activities and limited work requirements; they can deal with most social situations, including introductions; they can talk about concrete topics such as their own background, family, and interests, work, travel, and current events. At the Superior Level, they can state and defend opinions about current events and similar topics; they can participate in most formal and informal conversations on practical, social, professional, and abstract topics, on particular interests and special fields of interest.

Accuracy from Novice to Superior levels. At the Novice Level, accuracy is defined primarily as *intelligibility* because few if any grammar structures exist in the speech to warrant discussion of the precision of the message conveyed. Speakers at the Intermediate Level can be expected to make many errors even in constructions which are quite simple and common, with frequent errors in pronunciation and grammar. They are intelligible to a native speaker accustomed to dealing with foreigners. At the Advanced Level, they are joining sentences in limited discourse; they have good control of morphology of the language (in inflected languages) and of the most frequently used syntactic structures; and they usually handle elementary constructions quite accurately. They do not yet have thorough or confident control of grammar, and some miscommunication still takes place. They are, however, understandable to native speakers *not* used to dealing with foreigners. At the Superior Level, there are only occasional errors in low-frequency structures, occasional errors in the most complex frequent structures, and sporadic errors in basic structures. Errors never interfere with understanding and rarely disturb the native speaker. Control of grammar is good.

Materials for the Novice Level

What becomes very clear when one analyzes the speech of a Novice-Level speaker is that vocabulary is the essential feature that allows any form of communication whatsoever. In addition, pronunciation must be sufficiently accurate in that a few words and phrases at the speaker's disposal must be intelligible. One can easily imagine him or her using many gestures to accompany these words when trying to function in the target culture. Consequently, there is no functioning on the linguistic level, and language does not allow this speaker to accomplish any tasks.

What, then, would be the most appropriate materials to begin language study? First, the subject areas mentioned above are usually presented in the first few chapters of any textbook. Although limited communication depends mostly on the vocabulary, this is not to suggest that grammar is ignored at this level. For example, students are exposed to the present tense of regular verbs; they learn very common adjectives and adverbs, question verbs and negation; they are exposed to question forms (particularly yes/no questions), but when put into the situation of trying to have a conversation, these elements are still very unstable and may not surface with accuracy. These are students who may score 100 percent on a paper-and-pencil achievement test but whose language is limited to stock phrases and memorized sentences.

At first glance, it may seem that such limited language ability does not permit the use of particularly creative materials. However, at the most concrete levels and because their memory can retain much more than isolated words, students can acquire even idiomatic expressions when these are treated as lexical items. For example, very early in every textbook students are introduced to the polite form of a request "I would like." In this instance, all they need to add to this phrase are other words they have learned in order to communicate an idea. If we ask ourselves when we are most likely, in reality, to use the phrase "I would like," the situations we identify will suggest some of the materials we can create. In real discourse, the polite request is used in stores, cafés, and restaurants, when buying train tickets, when changing money, when introducing someone; and it can be used with a noun or an infinitive. The best sources for this basic survival language are the real objects associated with the situations described—packaging from products; labels from clothing; advertisements; foods; train, bus, and plane tickets; metro tickets, and catalogs from department stores. All of these realia supply a sufficiently wide vocabulary for students to be able to pick and choose and, although everyone in the class may be held responsible for a core vocabulary, individualization is possible through the definition of likes, dislikes, needs, hopes, and expectations.

Another source of information and materials is the imagination. What do we do first when we meet someone? What do we talk about in relatively superficial situations? The answers come readily to mind. First, we are likely to say "Hello" and introduce ourselves. We might make statements about the weather, particularly if it is exceptionally cold, hot, or beautiful. Then we are likely to move to autobiographical information, asking questions about the other person's life and supplying information about our own. As a general rule, it is always easier to arrive at communicative activities if we first take time to reflect on our experience and reality. Although this type of material will be presented at the very beginning of language learning, it is not going to become usable in a functional way until the Intermediate Level. Or to look at it from a different point of view, when these elements become stable, the student is likely to be near or in the Intermediate Level of proficiency.

The key for visuals at the Novice Level is that they must contain illustrations of as many objects (items) as possible. Since students have not yet reached the creative stage of language use, they rely very heavily on enumeration. The collage representing semantic fields (Maiguashca, 10) is particularly helpful. When dealing with family, foods, or any vocabulary group, the vocabulary can be taught in such a way that students realize from the outset that words have meaning only in relation to other words, that word families exist, that opposites help to define synonyms, and so forth. Students will learn very quickly that they should always look for alternative ways to say something, and as they progress in their language study, the habit of circumlocution will become more firmly established.

Although the ability to handle survival situations is characteristic of the Intermediate Level, the Novice speaker should be introduced to simulations as soon as enough simple connected language exists. For example, a situation card may look like this:

Play the role of waiter or student in the following situation. The student orders what he or she wishes to drink; the waiter brings the wrong beverage.

Modèle: Le Garçon: Vous désirez?
        L'Etudiante: Un thé au lait, s'il vous plaît.
        Le Garçon: Voilà, Madame ... un thé au citron.
        L'Etudiante: Non, Monsieur ... un thé au lait.
        Le Garçon: Ah, pardon, Madame, un thé au lait.
        L'Etudiante: Merci, Monsieur.
        Le Garçon: Je vous en prie, Madame.
[Bragger and Rice, 2, p. 6.]

(Waiter: What can I get you? Student: Tea with milk, please. Waiter: Here it is, Madam ... a tea with lemon. Student: No, sir ... tea with milk. Waiter: Excuse me, Madam ... a tea with milk. Student: Thank you. Waiter: You're welcome.)

This particular situation is presented in the target language to accustom students to the idea of a simulation. It is also very structured so that they have the chance to practice a particular combination of words over and over. The only thing they need to supply is the drink they wish to order. Such a directed situation is very useful at the precreative stage of language use. Once the structures are in place, the situation will become more open-ended.

You and a friend meet at a café.

1. Say hello to each other.
2. Order something to drink.
3. When the waiter (waitress) brings the wrong drink, correct him or her.
4. Say "thank you" when the right drink is brought to you.
5. When the two of you have finished your drink, say "goodbye" to each other.

If the first few situations do not contain a model in the target language, they must be presented very simply, and the structures and lexical content must be controlled as much as possible.

Find a person in the class to whom you have not yet introduced yourself.

1. Say hello.
2. Introduce yourself.

3. Ask how he or she is.
4. Ask his or her age.

Now introduce your new friend to someone else in the class.

The card may also direct the student to get specific information from another student.

Talk to one of your classmates and get the following information:

1. Name
2. Address
3. Phone number
4. Age

Once this information has been obtained, students can either report back to the entire class or exchange the information with another couple.

Additional materials for the Novice-Level speaker continue to stress the acquisition of vocabulary and simple structures. Newspaper headlines related to the semantic fields already encountered can be created. Slides and transparencies (e.g., cartoon frames without bubbles) can illustrate a simple series of actions. Finally, much can be created by the students themselves. An ad or collage prepared by students for homework allows them to show in pictures the vocabulary they would like to learn, their preferences, their interests. Instructors can then use these visuals as the basis for a class lesson giving students the additional satisfaction of having their work recognized and integrated into the classroom procedures.

Autobiographical information is most frequently provided when one first meets someone. Also we are always being asked to fill out forms such as nametags, luggage tags, driver's license, application forms, computer dating forms, lost-and-found forms, bills, class schedules, employment forms, and so forth. Once the information has been filled in, students can then move from the initial first person speech to the third person by describing someone else in the class. They can determine what they have in common, using the first person plural ("We are all students; many of us are eighteen years old; we all study Spanish and Geography.")

Materials for the Intermediate Level

From a grammatical point of view, the Intermediate-Level speaker is able to use the present indicative of regular verbs, some high-frequency irregular verbs, and the immediate future. However, many errors should still be expected, particularly with irregular verbs. At this point, there is a clear concept of gender, number, and subject-verb agreement, although many errors are likely to occur. Greater use is being made of modifiers, particularly articles and their contractions, possessive adjectives, and adverbs. Idiomatic expressions for weather, age, personal characteristics, and needs now exist in the active language. From the point of view of syntax, correct positioning of the most commonly used adjectives can now be expected.

When speaking of contexts at the Intermediate Level, we refer to survival situations typically encountered by the tourist in the foreign culture. These include getting food (restaurant, café, market); getting lodging (hotel, boardinghouse, youth hostel); traveling (various means of transportation, getting tickets, making reservations); telling time; making purchases; making simple transactions in the post office, bank, or pharmacy; greeting people and taking leave; speaking simply about future plans (immediate future); talking about family and friends; talking simply about self; and using numbers up to 1000 to be able to accomplish some of these tasks (dealing with money, for example).

These contexts clearly indicate that the scope of language now makes it possible to upgrade materials and to insist on accuracy in structures that before were unstable or nonexistent. In order to cope with survival situations, for example, students must be able to ask and answer questions. Most important, students are now creating with the language, a concept that merits some explanation because of its apparent vagueness. If the Novice speaker works primarily with memorized materials, this means that he or she repeats chunks of language without variation, using the interlocutor's questions as the springboard for the answers. The Intermediate speaker, on the other hand, although largely still working with memorized materials, is able to recombine them into personally meaningful messages. Language can be individualized as students become increasingly adaptable to a variety of contexts. They are capable of generalizing from the language they learned for one situation and applying it to another. Creating with the language, therefore, means increasing one's linguistic flexibility.

In analyzing the speech of Intermediate- to Superior-Level speakers, it is helpful to take into account the relative contribution model presented by Clifford and Higgs (7). According to the model, five linguistic factors contribute to speech: vocabulary, grammar, pronunciation, fluency, and sociolinguistic factors. At the level of the Educated Native Speaker, these factors contribute 20 percent each to make up the total speech act. At lower levels, each of the factors has a different weight depending on the proficiency of the speaker. As has been pointed out, vocabulary is definitely the dominating feature in speech at the Novice Level. The Intermediate Level, as defined in the relative contribution model, still shows the clear dominance of vocabulary as the major contributing factor to communication. When broken down by percentages, vocabulary contributes 45 percent to speech, pronunciation 18 percent, grammar 25 percent, fluency 7 percent, and the sociolinguistic factor 5 percent. By *sociolinguistic* is meant the ability to adjust language according to contexts in a culturally authentic way. It is understandable, therefore, that although the Intermediate speaker may know the difference between the informal *tu* and the formal *vous* in French, little else is present in speech to demonstrate cultural authenticity—hence, the almost insignificant contribution (5 percent) of the sociolinguistic factor at this level. Although the relative contribution model should not be taken as an absolute, it can help us to determine the most appropriate materials for each proficiency level and to become aware of what we can expect from the speakers at each level.

The most important consideration in choosing materials for the Intermediate Level is that they provide students with ample opportunity to create with the language. To do this, students must be accorded time, they must be allowed to work without constant supervision of the teacher, and they must be put into situations that are neither too structured nor too open-ended. At this level, students still need guidance, and the situation card is an ideal way to provide both guidance and freedom in expression. If appropriate situations are not already present in the textbook, they can easily be created for each chapter, with the context changing according to the chapter topics. For example, a situation card pertaining to a chapter on clothing might read:

> Go to the department store, choose an outfit for a particular occasion, and discuss size, color, and price with the salesperson. Your outfit should include shoes.

Upgrading the situation to include a complication, the same context can be presented in the following way:

> You're in the clothing department of a store to buy a blue sports jacket. There is only one jacket left in your size, but when you reach for it, you find out that another person also wants it. Both of you give the salesperson reasons why he or she should sell the jacket to you. [Bragger and Rice, 2, p. 311.]

It is clear that students cannot simply translate these situations but rather must communicate the ideas presented in them as best as they can within the scope of their language ability. Each student will probably have a different way of approaching the problem and this is where true creativity comes into play.

Numerous classroom activities have been created and published over the last few years, such that the work of instructors need not be particularly overwhelming. In addition to activities presented in textbooks, ancillary materials such as teacher's editions, instructor's manuals, tapes, etc. add to the wealth of materials. Meaningful communication is at the heart of many activities texts [see Moskowitz (11), Stevick (19), Schulz (16),

Westphal (20), Savignon and Berns (15), Smith (17), Guntermann and Phillips (4), Sadow (14), and Macdonald and Rogers-Gordon (9)]. Another useful source of information for the foreign language instructor is the many ESL texts that have appeared on the market. Because they tend to be organized along the functional-notional lines, they provide activities that can be incorporated easily into the foreign language classroom. One such example is the series *Lifelines 1, 2, 3, 4: Coping Skills in English* by Foley and Pomann (3), where students progress systematically from "Hello and Goodbye" (Chapter 1, *Lifelines 1*) to "Personal Information: Giving information about yourself during a job interview; Writing a résumé" (Chapter 14, *Lifelines 4*).

At the Intermediate Level, small-group work can begin and is very successful in fostering communication. Planning a trip, a party, the building of a house, etc. can be done in groups of four or five, with the results reported back to the entire class. Although the teacher is not with any of the groups unless questions are raised, the process of reporting back allows ample time for correction to take place after the report has been made. If lexical, grammatical, and structural lessons flow naturally from the statements made by students, this supports Rivers' contention that skill-getting and skill-using should flow naturally one from the other without stated lines of demarcation (12, 13). In every activity, students should be held accountable for what they have done or said, so that the end result of accurate communication can be achieved. As the flow of communication becomes easier, the correctness of speech must be increased progressively.

Materials for the Advanced Level

An Advanced-Level speaker should be considered as someone who speaks the language quite well, someone who could live on the economy in the target culture and work in a fairly routine job that does not demand a great deal of improvisation or present unknown situations. A percentage breakdown of the relative contribution chart indicates that pronunciation contributes 10 percent to effective communication, vocabulary 39 percent, grammar 38 percent, fluency 8 percent, and the sociolinguistic factor 5 percent. The most significant shift we note here is that the contribution of grammar, i.e., accuracy, has increased dramatically since the Intermediate Level. This, in turn, supports Higgs' (6, p. 7) contention that in order to arrive at this level, systematic error correction must occur from the very beginning of language study, and that if students are to rise to the Advanced Level, accuracy must have a prominent place in their language learning. In terms of accuracy, the Advanced-Level speaker can now be understood by a native speaker of the language who is *not* accustomed to dealing with foreigners. Fluency and the sociolinguistic factors have remained stable since the Intermediate Level, showing no marked increase in contribution to speech. This is to be expected since these are the elements that usually keep a person from sounding like a native speaker even though communication is already effectively managed.

The most important factor in the proficiency description is that the Advanced-Level speaker is able to *narrate and describe in present, past, and future time.* This indicates that, unlike the Intermediate speaker who still essentially communicates in sentences, the Advanced speaker is able to speak in paragraphs and convey the notion of time fairly accurately. The word *time* is used in this descriptor because, at this level, it is acceptable for someone to convey the future by using such expressions as "I plan to . . . ," "I expect to . . . ," "I hope to . . . ," "I'm going to . . . ," wherever such expressions are possible in a given language. In French, for example, the use of the true future tense is not required until the Superior-Level, in part because it has been noted that this is not a high-frequency tense in the daily spoken language. If the French themselves favor the immediate future in conversation, then it would seem unreasonable for us to expect our students to acquire habits that the French tend to avoid. There should never be a question of making students more French than the French, more Spanish than the Spanish, or more German than the Germans. To return to our example of the future tense, the Educated Native Speaker of French is, of course, able to use it if he or she chooses to do so. Consequently, as learners of French move into the Superior Level and, therefore, closer to the Educated Native Speaker, they must also acquire the ability to use the future tense.

For purposes of materials development, the notions of description and narration are crucial to a change in focus. Grammatically, this implies that students are now able to use connectors such as relative pronouns fairly accurately, that they have added many function words to their language, that their use of modifiers has increased, and that they can begin, continue, and end a story. Control of elements such as possessive and demonstrative adjectives, which are unstable at the lower levels, is now expected most of the time. Object pronouns should be used correctly and with regularity to keep narration and description from becoming repetitive. Prepositions should be in place, and the notion of negation should have been developed to include the concepts of *never, no one, no longer,* and so forth.

All of the above suggest that we must now concentrate on giving these students ample opportunity for narration and description. It further indicates that extensive work needs to be done with the concepts of past, present, and future time. Most important, it suggests that instructors must allow students to speak without interruption of the language they are trying to create and the story they are trying to tell. Constant interruption under these circumstances will lead to disjointed discourse, discrete sentences, and little sense of continuity. Yet correction must still be a part of the learning process, so activities must still be guided, and systematic follow-up for correction must have its place.

The materials suggested earlier—e.g., ads, pictures, cartoons, slides, newspapers, and magazines—will now be used somewhat differently since students are asked to engage in lengthier discourse. One may ask them to describe something in detail or to create a story with invented or imagined details. Autobiographical elements used earlier in mostly question/answer form should be expanded and elaborated. It is now possible to add current events, with students recounting the details of a story they heard on the radio or read in a newspaper. Those who are not familiar with the current political scene (as many students are not), can concentrate on what is happening on campus, student elections, controversial issues, or the student newspaper. What is important here is not that the course suddenly be transformed into a political science course, but that students acquire the skills to function in a variety of contexts requiring the ability to inform someone about something. The following are specific techniques allowing them to do so.

Reporting back what has been heard or read. First, students need to be taught the linguistic elements commonly needed to report back effectively. This can be accomplished initially through short utterances: " 'Mary, what did you do yesterday?' 'I stayed at home and did my homework. I also helped my parents in the garden.' " " 'Paul, tell us what Mary did yesterday.' 'Mary said that she stayed at home and did her homework. She also helped her parents in the garden.' " In other words, students need to become adept at using introductory statements such as "she said," "she explained," and so forth. From there, they can be asked to gather information from other students and to combine this information into a short paragraph for reporting to the rest of the class. In some instances, they can be the observers in a group, or the recording secretary, who is responsible for summarizing what has been said. Also, students must be able to bring their narration or description to a smooth closure and not simply stop speaking at the end of the last sentence. In addition, the ability to state opinion becomes increasingly important since students need to learn how to comment on what was said using appropriate opinion statements.

Selling something to someone. Students try to convince someone of the superior quality of the product they are trying to sell. This includes the ability to make comparisons and use the superlative and many descriptive adjectives. Advertisements for this activity may be chosen either by the instructor or the student.

Teaching the teacher. You, the instructor, must choose a subject area with which you are not very familiar but that you know is well known by students, for example, rock music or a particular singer, sports, dances, movies, etc. In small groups or as a class, students prepare to teach you as much as possible about their subject. They will usually prepare this ahead of time so that they can support what they are saying with examples (taped songs, visuals, demonstrations). The advantage of choosing topics truly unfamiliar to the teacher is that students know they are not simply repeating things already well known to the teacher. In this instance they are the experts.

Short lectures. Pick a subject that is not commonly an area of expertise for most teenagers (e.g., classical music). Present a concise, five-minute speech about the topic and then have students summarize what they have learned. As students become accustomed to this procedure, it is important that you include opinion statements so that they learn to reflect your feelings about the particular topic. Note-taking may or may not be allowed.

Semantic fields. Word association that leads to short sentences at the Novice and Intermediate levels leads to more extensive narration at the Advanced Level. In fact, brainstorming a word results in the creation of stories, factual or invented. For example, the word *green* may first recall a single word. Then students have to explain why they made the particular association, telling the story that is connected with it. Words such as *money, work, vacation,* or *parents* are particularly useful, in that they elicit not only facts but also many personal feelings.

Comparing with autobiographical information. Students compare their upbringing and childhood to that of their parents or grandparents. They then explain what they intend to do once they have children of their own. This allows them to highlight the problems parents have in raising children today, the problems that are likely to exist in the future, and the ones they would probably not have had twenty or thirty years ago. At the same time, students are revealing a great deal about themselves as individuals.

Situation cards with a complication. The situation cards used at the Intermediate Level were planned to give students the ability to get into, through, and out of a routine, expected situation. At the Advanced Level, students must now cope with a problem that presents itself unexpectedly. To judge how effectively communication takes place, it is useful to give the situation card to only one student, while his or her partner is left in the dark about what is going to happen. The partner's understanding of the situation helps to determine how well the task was handled. It also obliges the second student to react spontaneously to the situation. Another interesting variation consists of giving each student a card, but neither knows what is on the other's card. Neither person knows therefore how the other will react, thus making improvisation an imperative.

Summarizing an article or piece of writing. Each student reads a short article as homework. In class he or she is given two minutes to recount the essence of the article. If the same work has been read by the entire class, the rest of the students are then invited to comment on the summary, add to it, disagree on the interpretation of the message, or agree with the points that have been made. If different articles are read by each student, the rest of the class may ask questions for clarification or additional information.

Debate. Students are divided into groups of five, with two arguing for and two arguing against the topic question, and one serving as the moderator. Topics should be sufficiently controversial to ensure a lively debate (e.g., the drinking age, capital punishment, etc.). Each member of the team chooses a particular aspect of the topic and is allowed two or three minutes to present the point of view. The result will be a short paragraph. When all the members of the debate team have made their statements, they are invited to challenge statements made by the opposing faction. Finally, the rest of the class asks the panel questions for clarification or commentary. A vote can then be taken to determine which side presented its arguments more effectively. The moderator is the timekeeper and directs follow-up discussion.

Description of activities. Since it is assumed that the Advanced-Level speaker can describe his or her activities on a typical or particular day, this should be a regular part of class activities. Expectations would include correct use of the reflexive in the languages that necessitate it and accuracy in present as well as past and future tenses. Since daily activities often do not vary greatly among students in the same age group, the question of how these activities vary on holidays, vacations, and weekends can add the variety needed to keep the descriptions interesting. To reduce the amount of time devoted to this activity, students can be instructed to get the information from their neighbor during the minutes *before* class begins. The instructor can then arbitrarily choose one of them to give the information thus obtained to the rest of the class. This procedure has the additional advantage of getting students accustomed to using the target language outside of class and to help them realize that it is not only used during the precise time of the class period. They should already be busy communicating with each other when the teacher enters the class. Periodically, during the semester or year, the information they are to get can be changed.

Film. At the Advanced Level, students should be able to retell stories they have seen or heard. If films are not readily available to instructors, storytelling can be based on movies students have seen. If a target-language film is being shown on campus or in town, students can be required to see it so that everyone will have a common basis for discussion.

Current events. At regularly paced intervals, students are asked to talk about an article they have read in the newspaper or a story they have heard on the radio or seen on television. In addition to reinforcing speaking skills, this activity helps students to inculcate the habit of informing themselves about what is happening in the world. Because foreign language newspapers or news broadcasts are not always available, it is also valuable for students to acquire the habit of reading the newspapers their parents read or make a habit of listening to radio or television news. The important result is that they will acquire the ability to recount in the target language what they have read, heard, or seen. If one of these news stories happens to concern the target culture, so much the better.

Integration with other subjects studied in school. Description and narration can be based on a book students have read in English class, a composition they have heard in music class, a painting they have studied in art history, or a problem they discussed in social studies. The added advantage to this type of integration with the target language is that students will begin to appreciate the interrelationships of subjects and will understand them not as isolated courses of study but rather as integral parts of the human experience.

Materials for the Superior Level

The percentage breakdown represented in the relative contribution model indicates that pronunciation at the Superior Level now contributes 5 percent to total speech production, vocabulary 27 percent, grammar 45 percent, fluency 15 percent, and the sociolinguistic factor 8 percent. The emphasis has now decidedly moved to grammatical accuracy, and this is the factor that distinguishes the speech of a Superior-Level speaker.

What should students be prepared for in order to successfully complete the tasks characteristic of this level? First, the Superior rating represents *professional competency* in the language. The individual no longer simply lives on the economy, but is able to be an independent individual within the target culture. Although he or she will still be recognized as a foreigner, most tasks likely to be required can be accomplished with relative ease. The speaker should be able to improvise in unfamiliar situations, use circumlocution to disguise some of the lacunae still existing in the language, hypothesize using conditional sentences, support opinion, state the pros and cons, present differing points of view, and react correctly to the nuances of almost any discussion. A Superior-Level speaker is a full conversational partner who contributes completely to the discussion, at least linguistically. Since, at this point, students are at the most mature stages of their formal language learning, the range and use of materials are virtually limitless. Students must be given the opportunity to converse as much as possible, with refinements and corrections made less frequently than was done earlier.

Situations. These are now designed to be unfamiliar, with some vocabulary items that students have probably not encountered before. The instructor should, however, be fairly certain that circumlocution is within their capability so that linguistic breakdown does not occur. Students should understand that they may not know every word in the situation but that they should do the best they can to communicate the message, working around the word and finding ways to replace it. If they have been trained from the very first course to say things in different ways, they will not have a great deal of difficulty grasping this concept and they should get along quite well.

> During a severe thunderstorm you discover that the water is pouring into your basement and that your floor drains are plugged up. When you try to call the plumber, you find out that your phone is out. Go to your neighbor, explain the situation, ask to borrow some brooms and buckets, and ask if you can use the phone to call the plumber. Ask your neighbor if he or she could come and help you sweep the water out of the basement.

This situation is one that students are not likely to have experienced, and it contains vocabulary that is not usually taught. In short, it requires them to do the best they can to get the help they need.

Because the number of contexts has been increased to include work-related and career-oriented considerations at the Superior Level, it is important to create materials and strategies that allow students to enter into the type of language that reflects their professional interests. This may include business terminology, social work, literature, teaching, technical translation, and so forth. Since most students do not yet find themselves in a real professional situation but rather in courses preparing them for the future, discussion of more technical aspects of other courses is one way to approach these topics. It is not really a question of becoming too technical but of being able to discuss basic concepts in lay terms. One does not have to be a doctor to talk about what doctors do, nor does one have to be a lawyer to describe the most common professional concerns of the lawyer. Perhaps more detail can be demanded when students are addressing the profession of their choice, particularly since other course work has probably given them a special expertise in their chosen field.

Hypothesizing and supporting opinion are the main distinguishing features of the Superior Level. However, before conversation flows freely, much practice is needed to solidify conditional tenses and sentences. This may be done with exercises of sentence completion, where either the first element or the resulting clause is given. To develop accurate habits at this stage, the repetition of the clause in conjunction with the response is important.

Examples: If I could relive my life . . .
If I could spend an afternoon with the president
of the U.S. . . .
If I had children . . .
. . . I would have gone to another university.
. . . I would go to China.
. . . I would not lend her the money.

Problem solving. A series of problems is presented and students have to give advice to another person or group ("If I were you, I would . . ."). The person or group receiving the advice may ask for clarification ("When would you . . . , why would you . . . , where would you . . ."). If the problems are designed well, they will represent some concerns and situations in which students may one day find themselves or have already experienced. Topics of particular interest are: getting a job, not getting a job, responses to hypothetical interview questions, unemployment, to have or not to have a family, how children should be raised, what you would do if you found out that your company requires you to travel extensively and therefore leave your family, etc.

Radio and TV broadcasts. Students may prepare presentations, including weather, sports, and so forth. A more challenging experience consists of turning on the television set in the classroom, turning off the sound, and having students invent the dialogue or act as the announcers as the program progresses. Programs that are particularly useful for this type of activity are soap operas, cartoons, and sports events.

Conversational fillers. One important aspect of real conversation is knowing *how* to hesitate, to disguise the searching for a word or structure. In part, this is accomplished with conversational fillers or hesitation words. Every teacher knows how difficult it is to introduce these into student speech so that they will emerge correctly and at the appropriate times. To begin with, the fillers must be part of a relatively structured situation. For example, a small group is given a particular topic to discuss. At the same time, each student in the group is given a card with a number of fillers and is instructed to use each one at least once during the course of the discussion. The same can be done with idiomatic expressions used to state opinion or with any other recurring expression that is not context-specific.

Taped conversations used as a basis for the class lesson. A group of students is asked to tape ten minutes of a discussion on a given topic or a topic of their choice. The tape is then used on the same or subsequent day as the basis for the lesson. The conversation is analyzed grammatically, lexically, and from a cultural point of view. The instructor and students make suggestions and corrections, find different ways of expressing the same idea, work with vocabulary groups, analyze the preciseness with which ideas were expressed. This activity will be upgraded or downgraded automatically because students will always express themselves at the level that is most natural to them. It can thus be used at almost any level, even when the expression of ideas is still very basic. Students enjoy this activity because they know their contribution determines the lesson; they hear their own voices, they are praised for what they do well, and they learn what they can improve.

Interpretation, analysis, and criticism. One important characteristic of Superior-Level speakers is that they deal more comfortably with abstract concepts, allowing them to discuss controversial subjects, philosophical or moral problems, and the intangibles of feeling. At this point, for example, the teacher can play a classical composition and ask students to describe the feelings the music evokes in them. Examples of related activities are the discussion of various levels of meaning in a literary text such as a poem; the interpretation and criticism of a speech delivered by a political candidate or figure; the discussion of stereotypes, cultural differences, and similarities; and the expression of reactions to stressful or happy situations. Since very few contexts are off limits at the Superior Level, it is generally easier to promote discussion providing, of course, that the contexts are somehow of interest to students.

Homework Assignments and the Development of Oral Proficiency

Perhaps the most difficult task facing a teacher is how to have students continue conversational practice outside of class. The following suggestions require little or no teacher preparation and they enable students to practice what has been learned in class. Too often, speaking the target language occurs only during the three to five weekly hours of class. With twenty to thirty students in the average class, it is clear that each student will have relatively little time to work on this skill.

Conversational partners. At the beginning of the year or semester, students who live near each other are paired up as conversational partners. They are instructed to spend two half-hour periods per week in conversation with each other. Until they become comfortable with this practice, they may be given specific subjects of discussion. They are then asked to report back to the teacher and/or the class, to explain any conclusions they have reached and why, to explain when and why they had problems expressing a particular idea. A different and perhaps more efficient check is to have them tape their conversations to be turned in. Suggestions and corrections are then recorded directly onto the tape by the teacher. It is important to note not only the negative features but also the strengths in order to make the conversational partnership a positive experience. The two students then listen to the instructor's comments together and consciously work on incorporating corrections and suggestions into the next conversation.

Taped homework. Among the many assignments that can be done on cassette are the following: interview someone, answer a series of questions, present a point of view on a problem, tape a skit with other students, read a text, give a short lecture. For regular, direct communication with the teacher, students can be asked to keep a taped journal, an audio cassette on which they record anything that comes to mind, such as a problem, a request for information, a request for an opinion or any other message they wish to transmit to the teacher. The instructor then answers directly on the cassette. This is a variation on the dialogue journal (18), and is a more personal, individual means of communication.

This type of homework is particularly important in a conversation course, where too frequently homework consists exclusively of reading or writing, skills that contribute only indirectly to the development of oral proficiency. The more often students are given the opportunity to engage in meaningful conversation, the more feedback they receive on their way of expressing ideas, the more likely it is that their language skills will improve.

Summary

In this chapter we have attempted to describe some of the many activities and possible materials that may be used to develop oral proficiency. Most of these activities involve the other skills—reading, listening, speaking, culture—although in these instances they serve primarily as supporting skills for oral communication. This emphasis on the oral skill does not suggest, however, that speaking is or should be considered more important than writing or the receptive skills. In terms of proficiency, it is simply the one that has been worked with first, the one that has a proficiency evaluation firmly in place, the one that has been developed with greater difficulty in past years. With the introduction of the Oral Proficiency Interview into academia has come the realization that perhaps too little attention has been paid to the development of oral proficiency in the past, that too little has been known about its place in the classroom, that it has been simpler to talk about than to put appropriate techniques into action. Rather than overshadowing the development of proficiency in the other skills, speaking is now on a more equal footing in pedagogical considerations and practice.

The basic principles proposed for speaking activities and materials may also be followed for the other skills. The ACTFL Provisional Proficiency Guidelines are again the best descriptors of what may be expected at the various levels and the contexts that are appropriate. Whenever possible, it is advisable to devote some time in each class period to the specific skills, upgrading materials as necessary, moving from the factual and concrete to the abstract, from words to sentences to paragraphs, from survival situations to the unfamiliar. Materials should be designed to challenge students to progress beyond themselves, to help them realize their potential, to give them the opportunity to work with and acquire the authentic language as it is spoken and written in the target culture.

References, Materials Development for the Proficiency-Oriented Classroom

1. *ACTFL Provisional Proficiency Guidelines.* Hastings-on-Hudson, NY: American Council on the Teaching of Foreign Languages, 1982.
2. Bragger, Jeannette D., and Donald B. Rice. *Allons-y! Le Français par étapes.* Boston: Heinle and Heinle, 1984.
3. Foley, Barbara, and Howard Pomann. *Lifelines, Coping Skills in English.* New York: Regents, 1981.
4. Guntermann, Gail, and June K. Phillips. *Functional-Notional Concepts: Adapting the Foreign Language Textbook.* Language in Education: Theory and Practice, no. 44. Washington, DC: Center for Applied Linguistics, 1982.
5. Hammerly, Hector. *Synthesis in Second Language Teaching.* Blaine, WA: Second Language Publications, 1982.
6. Higgs, Theodore V. "Language Teaching and the Quest for the Holy Grail," pp. 1–9 in Theodore V. Higgs, ed., *Teaching for Proficiency, the Organizing Principle.* The ACTFL Foreign Language Education series, vol. 15. Lincolnwood, IL: National Textbook Co., 1984.
7. _____, and Ray Clifford. "The Push Toward Communication," pp. 57–79 in Theodore V. Higgs, ed., *Curriculum, Competence, and the Foreign Language Teacher.* The ACTFL Foreign Language Education Series, vol. 13. Lincolnwood, IL: National Textbook Co., 1982.
8. Liskin-Gasparro, Judith E. "The ACTFL Proficiency Guidelines: A Historical Perspective," pp. 11–42 in Theodore V. Higgs, ed., *Teaching for Proficiency, the Organizing Principle.* The ACTFL Foreign Language Education Series, vol. 15. Lincolnwood, IL: National Textbook Co., 1984.
9. Macdonald, Marion, and Sue Rogers-Gordon. *Action Plans, 80 Student-Centered Language Activities.* Rowley, MA: Newbury House, 1984.
10. Maiguashca, Raffaella Uslenghi. "Semantic Fields: Towards a Methodology for Teaching Vocabulary in the Second-Language Classroom," pp. 274–97. *The Canadian Modern Language Review* 40, 2 (1984).
11. Moskowitz, Gertrude. *Caring and Sharing in the Foreign Language Class.* Rowley, MA: Newbury House, 1978.
12. Rivers, Wilga M. *A Practical Guide to the Teaching of French.* New York: Oxford University Press, 1975.
13. _____. *Communicating Naturally in a Second Language.* Cambridge: Cambridge University Press, 1983.
14. Sadow, Stephen A. *Idea Bank, Creative Activities for the Language Class.* Rowley, MA: Newbury House, 1982.

15. Savignon, Sandra J., and Margie S. Berns. *Initiatives in Communicative Language Teaching.* Reading, MA: Addison-Wesley, 1984.
16. Schulz, Renate A., ed. *Teaching for Communication.* Report of Central States Conference on the Teaching of Foreign Languages. Lincolnwood, IL: National Textbook Co., 1976.
17. Smith, Stephen M. *The Theater Arts and the Teaching of Second Languages.* Reading, MA: Addison-Wesley, 1984.
18. Staton, Jana. "Dialogue Journals: A New Tool for Teaching Communication." *ERIC/CLL News Bulletin* 6, 2 (March 1983):3.
19. Stevick, Earl W. *Teaching and Learning Languages.* Cambridge: Cambridge University Press, 1982.
20. Westphal, Patricia B., ed. *Strategies for Foreign Language Teaching.* Report of Central States Conference on the Teaching of Foreign Languages. Lincolnwood, IL: National Textbook Co., 1984.

4

From Achievement toward Proficiency through Multi-Sequence Evaluation

Sally Sieloff Magnan
University of Wisconsin-Madison

Introduction

The proficiency movement is having a major impact on our profession. It is already generating considerable discussion, interest, and concern. It promises an increase in the accountability of our profession, through standardized evaluation of how our students can function in the foreign language; and an improvement of our curriculum, through a restructuring of course goals to include functional, as well as cognitive objectives.

The proficiency movement is perhaps best known through the Oral Proficiency Interview (OPI), a structured conversation between one candidate and one evaluator lasting from about ten to thirty minutes. This OPI procedure is based on the oral interview of the government language schools, first developed during the Second World War. It is rated globally, so that each candidate receives one of the following nine ratings, which describes the functions, content, and accuracy of the candidate's speech: Novice Low, Novice Mid, Novice High, Intermediate Low, Intermediate Mid, Intermediate High, Advanced, Advanced Plus, and Superior. (For

Sally Sieloff Magnan (Ph.D., Indiana University) is Assistant Professor of French at the University of Wisconsin-Madison, where she teaches language and methodology courses, coordinates lower-level courses, and supervises teaching assistants. Her articles and reviews have appeared in the *Modern Language Journal, Studies in Second Language Acquisition, French Review,* and the *Report of the Central States Conference on the Teaching of Foreign Languages.* She has been a trainer for oral proficiency testing in the IFLTA intensive workshops, the University of Minnesota 1984 Summer Proficiency Project, and in numerous familiarization workshops nationwide. She is a member of ACTFL, AATF, AAAL, AAUSC, and WAFLT.

a historical perspective on the development of the rating scale, see Liskin-Gasparro, 8.) Currently Oral Proficiency Interviews are being used or piloted for use in numerous institutions across the nation. Uses include test batteries for placement into university courses, for satisfying the foreign language requirement, and for certification of bilingual and foreign language teachers (see Freed, 4; Jiménez and Murphy, 6; and Liskin-Gasparro, 8).

The proficiency movement actually involves more than an oral test. Provisional proficiency guidelines have been written for all four skills (speaking, writing, reading, listening) and culture. Eventually there will be a set of testing procedures for each skill area, with plans currently underway in reading. In fairness, then, the proficiency movement should not be equated only with the OPI; nevertheless, it is the only test available at present and thus is the focal point of current discussion.

As classroom teachers become familiar with the proficiency movement and with the OPI, they often begin to look for ways to orient their teaching toward proficiency, that is, to make it more communicative and more oriented toward actual language use in the foreign culture. Teachers undoubtedly ask themselves questions such as the following: If my students will someday have to take the OPI, do I need to "teach to the test"? Are there philosophical problems in teaching to a test, especially an extracurricular test? If I wanted to prepare students for the OPI, how would I go about it, especially since it is an oral test and so much of my classwork is based on writing?

This chapter attempts to answer these questions. After arguing that it is indeed appropriate to organize classroom teaching and testing around the various elements of the OPI, a multi-sequence system for classroom evaluation will be proposed to help prepare students for greater functional use of the foreign language and thus for better performance on the OPI. Most examples will involve speaking, although the testing sequence proposed can be applied as well to writing, reading, and listening.

Philosophical Arguments for "Teaching to the Test" ⎯⎯⎯⎯

In order to discuss the philosophical issue of teaching to the test, we need to examine the key features of the OPI. First, the OPI is a testing procedure, providing a flexible, individualized assessment for each student, based on proficiency descriptions of different levels of functional linguistic ability. It is not, therefore, a "secure" test, where confidentiality would be necessary; since no two tests are the same, it would not be cheating to inform students about, and even to have them practice, the "test" in advance. Given the individuality of the OPI, there is no philosophical problem of fairness in allowing students prior exposure to the interview procedure.

Second, the OPI measures functional ability in the foreign language, that is, what students can do with the language rather than what they know about it. If we lead our students to be more successful users of French, Spanish, German, Russian, or whatever language, are we not attaining goals that we normally set for our classroom instruction?

In fact, the elements of the OPI are those we generally teach in class anyway. For example, on the Novice Level, candidates are asked to list objects, persons, and activities. On the Intermediate Level, candidates describe and narrate simply in present time, ask simple questions, and role-play common situations. On the Advanced Level, they narrate and describe in the past and future, compare, explain, and role-play more complicated situations in which it is often appropriate to ask, argue, plead, convince, or tactfully accept (and reject) the viewpoints of others. On the Superior Level, candidates support opinions, hypothesize, describe with precision, and role-play complex, unfamiliar situations with appropriate sociolinguistic distinctions and a wide range of linguistic functions.

In the OPI these functions are measured in accordance with the context in which they appear (topic or vocabulary areas) and the accuracy with which they are used (including sociolinguistic features, pronunciation, fluency, vocabulary, and especially grammar). Activities typically used in the OPI are also commonly found in the classroom: identifying objects and listing items in common semantic areas, asking and answering questions, speaking in monologue form at some length, and acting out role plays. The OPI is thus, at least in theory, appropriate both in content and in form to contemporary classroom teaching. In terms of classroom focus and course goals, as well as fairness, it should be philosophically acceptable to teach to the OPI.

If we are to accept the notion of teaching to the test, this would most probably include aligning graded classroom tests more closely with the OPI. Indeed, many scholars and teachers would argue that classroom tests should focus, at least in part, on functional and oral language use. Data by Nerenz suggests that, at least at the secondary level, teachers spend considerable class time on the speaking skill. She observed twenty middle school and high school teachers in southern Wisconsin and discovered that 24 percent of class time was devoted to oral activities, including warm-up exercises, pronunciation exercises, Gouin series, dialogues, and guided and free conversation (Nerenz, 9). Snyder points out that although, as Nerenz shows, teachers today have introduced a variety of creative and communicative classroom exercises into their lessons, many continue to test only knowledge of grammar and syntax and not ability to speak the language (Snyder, 18, p. 34). In order to test what we teach and expect, we must then offer more oral tests based on the activities and expectations of our classrooms. To the degree that the functional orientation and activities of the OPI are appropriate to our classrooms and to our expectations, it is not only fitting but also necessary that we teach and test to the OPI.

Types of Tests

In designing a plan by which we can lead students, through classroom exercises and tests, toward better performance on the OPI and, we hope, toward greater ability to use the foreign language in the target culture, it is useful to consider the types of tests currently available. Spolsky outlines a three-phase history of foreign language testing, many components of which are still used today. Prior to the 1950s, teachers had an "elitist" approach to testing, in that there was a general lack of concern for statistical analysis, objectivity, and reliability. This was the *prescientific era*: teachers felt that any test they designed was fine because they were the teachers. During this period, we saw mostly written tests, particularly involving translation. Under the influence of Lado and the structural-analytical approach to linguistic research in the 1950s, called the *psychometric-structuralist era,* tests emphasized grammatical features. The format was typically discrete-point, that is, a test that traditionally focuses attention on one point at a time within the context of a single sentence. In discrete-point testing, language is dissected into its component parts and examined piece by piece. Typical formats of discrete-point tests include multiple choice and fill-in-the-blank. Beginning in the late 1960s, during the *psycholinguistic-sociolinguistic era,* tests became more integrative, more global, in order to measure the total communicative aspect of language, including the social context. These tests are designed to evaluate language use in appropriate linguistic and sociolinguistic contexts, that is, to put it simply, in contextualized paragraphs. Whereas discrete items attempt to test linguistic knowledge one bit at a time, integrative tests attempt to assess a learner's capacity to use many bits simultaneously (Spolsky, 19; Howard, 5, p. 273; Oller, 11, p. 37; Wesche, 24, p. 55). As Clark points out, since the late 1970s when Spolsky's article was written, there has been an increasing interest and development in direct proficiency testing that requires the student to perform functionally oriented tasks in activities that approximate as closely as possible actual situations; tests such as the OPI fall in this final category (Clark, 3, p. 433).

The question raised by this historical perspective is, of course, which of these tests are best? That is, which are most likely to help students meet the objective of functional language use?

Achievement versus Proficiency Testing

In order to answer this question, we need to consider the goals of the test. Before all else, we must consider if the test measures proficiency or achievement. It is imperative to distinguish clearly between these two concepts.

Achievement tests are those we give for grades in the classroom. They are limited to course material. They are norm-referenced, that is, they are graded in terms of what we feel we can reasonably expect or in terms of the performance of other students. It is therefore possible, at least in theory, to give perfect grades on achievement tests, since they are based on limited amounts of knowledge that students have been taught. The grade assigned on an achievement test is generally determined by individually scored items. Individually scored items are usually necessary for achievement tests, since a main purpose of achievement testing is to provide specific feedback to both student and teacher.

In contrast, proficiency tests are not limited to course material. They are criterion-referenced, measuring the ability of each student (even at the most elementary stages) against an absolute standard; this is, in the case of the OPI, the Educated Native Speaker of the language. Proficiency tests are thus not appropriate tools for determining course grades, since they do not measure what the students have learned from the material they have been taught but rather how much of the language in its entirety they can use. Furthermore, proficiency tests, like the OPI, are generally rated globally, in accordance with their goal of providing an assessment of the candidate's overall linguistic ability.

We give achievement tests for a number of purposes other than assigning course grades: to assess the effectiveness of the syllabus, materials, and our teaching methods; to help us diagnose precise areas where students are having difficulty; to motivate students, albeit externally; and to give students periodic feedback throughout the learning process. We use proficiency tests for purposes that exceed the parameters of our particular classrooms: placement in subsequent courses, satisfaction of school requirements, and official certification, often part of the hiring or classification of employees.

Matching the Type of Test to the Purpose of the Test

All three of the test types described by Spolsky and the direct tests discussed by Clark have been used for testing both achievement and proficiency. In fact, there is currently no consensus on which type is best suited to which purpose. For example, researchers in test design such as Farhady and Oller disagree on whether or not discrete-point tests are as effective as integrative tests for measuring language proficiency (Oller, 12, pp. 137–38). With regard to measuring achievement, some scholars, such as Omaggio, believe that we should move away from the single-sentence (generally discrete-point) formats typically used in achievement testing toward "hybrid" tests, in which most of the items are open-ended and elicit sequential, naturalistic discourse (Omaggio, 13). Others agree with Clark in thinking that we should completely abandon discrete-point tests and even more integrative tests such as the cloze procedure, in favor of tests that better reflect real-life language use in situation (Clark, 3, p. 440). In either case, we are confronted with a revolution against traditional classroom testing.

The very nature of the achievement test would have to change, for if we are to heed Omaggio's advice, we could not simply retain our traditional tests, supplementing them in an ad hoc fashion with a few communicative items (Omaggio, 13, pp. 7–8).

Of course, not everyone advocates such a radical solution. Canale, for example, claims that we cannot simply rule out tests restricted to a single aspect of communication, such as vocabulary or grammatical form, nor can we legitimately rule out any specific testing method, such as multiple choice. Under the appropriate conditions, these test types are quite legitimate and, in fact, often recommended. Instead, Canale advocates matching the test format with the type of skill the test is to measure: using integrative, skill-oriented methods for assessing overall receptive and expressive skills, and using discrete-point, knowledge-oriented methods for assessing mastery of bits of knowledge (Canale, 2, p. 83). Valette and Disick make a similar suggestion in their subject-matter taxonomy that proposes using discrete-point tests to measure linguistic competence, represented in their stages "mechanical skills," "knowledge," and "transfer," and global tests to measure communicative competence, represented in their stage "communication" (Valette and Disick, 23, p. 41). This notion of matching the test to the task provides the rationale for the following multi-sequence system of achievement testing.

Multi-Sequence Evaluation

There is a natural progression in moving from achievement to proficiency. Insofar as a proficiency test, such as the OPI, measures abilities that we naturally desire for our students, we will want our achievement tests to prepare students for this proficiency test. Since the OPI measures functional language ability in a variety of contexts, we would be progressing toward our instructional objectives if our achievement tests helped prepare students for the OPI.

This does not mean that our classroom tests should involve the same content and be in the same format as the OPI. The skills needed in acquiring bits of language knowledge and individual linguistic forms, such as we teach in the beginning classroom, may be quite different from the skills needed in integrating these bits of knowledge into language use in situation. Different test formats are needed to evaluate most effectively and efficiently these different steps of the learning process.

Multi-sequence evaluation involves establishing a systematic progression or sequence for achievement tests that moves from the most restrictive word or sound level, through the more expanded utterance or basic sentence level, to an expanded level of relatively full discourse. In this way classroom tests would direct student learning through the memorization of forms to integrative and functional use of language in situation.

This proposed system of multi-sequence evaluation recalls Paulston's sequence for oral practice in the classroom (15), in which she advocates moving from mechanical questions involving automatic responses, through meaningful questions involving a single correct answer, to communicative questions that are open-ended, allowing many possible and extended answers. Just as each time we practice a new form or concept in our classes, we use a drill sequence to help students learn the new material and then integrate it into material already learned, so each time we evaluate students at a specific step of the learning process, we need to use a testing sequence to inform them and ourselves of the degree of mastery they have achieved.

We obviously make several passes in evaluation as we do in drilling. Valdman and others suggest that such successive passes are most useful if they are cyclic in nature, not merely reiterative, each pass reviewing old features that are likely to be forgotten and adding new ones. In cyclic ordering, grammatical features, for example, are not taught in monolithic blocks; rather, different subfeatures are targeted for different types of mastery at different points of instruction. A verb tense might first be targeted for passive recognition only, then for commitment to memory so that it could be reproduced; subsequently, it would be targeted for active use in highly structured contexts, and then for fully integrative use in a variety of environments (Valdman, 21, pp. 34–51). Multi-sequence evaluation attempts to incorporate the notions of sequence and cyclical ordering by offering a progressive system of testing that is cyclic in nature.

Within the cycle of achievement tests, a proficiency test such as the OPI may, of course, be given at any time. Performance will depend on how much of the language the students have mastered, on how much of the testing sequence they can do with ease. If the desired result is not attained on the proficiency test, the student returns to the classroom and reenters the study/achievement cycle, unless, of course, a nonacademic learning experience, such as study abroad, is advisable and possible.

Principles of multi-sequence evaluation

Seven principles of the proposed system of multi-sequence evaluation follow.

1. *Test formats should be suited to the particular task.* When isolated forms are being learned, discrete-point testing is most appropriate. When the focus of learning progresses to using learned forms in a limited, structured context, hybrid tests such as formats involving contextualized sentences and short paragraphs are appropriate. When highly integrative language use is the desired goal, testing should be open-ended and should approximate language use in sociolinguistically appropriate situations.

2. *The use of test formats should proceed along a continuum.* At first, isolated forms should be tested, using discrete-point items for recognition and then for production; items should become progressively more open-ended and integrative in relation to more functional teaching objectives.

3. *The continuum can be considered as having four key phases,* in each of which a variety of test types would be found: (1) *recognition phase,* testing recognition and differentiation of isolated forms using discrete-point formats; (2) *memory phase,* testing active production of isolated forms or memorized expressions using discrete-point formats; (3) *contextualized phase,* simultaneous testing of a variety of language forms and concepts as used in the context of sentences or short paragraphs; and (4) *discourse phase,* testing ability to use forms integratively to produce extended discourse.

4. *This testing sequence implies teaching for recognition or passive knowledge before active usage,* as is suggested by Terrell (20), Postovsky (16), and others. It naturally links reading to writing and listening to speaking. As this link suggests, multi-sequence evaluation can apply, with certain logical modifications, to all four skills, and ideally it should end in free integration of these skills.

5. *Grading in each phase of the sequence should be in accordance with the nature of the tasks involved.* Grading in the recognition and memory phases, therefore, can be quite objective since these phases are tested using discrete-point items. In grading items in the contextualized phase, we will need to consider more aspects, at least semantic content and grammatical form. In this phase, grading will still be mainly objective, with some subjective elements as necessary. In the discourse phase, where forms are used integratively to produce expanded discourse, we will want to consider function, content, and accuracy (the Functional Trisection of the OPI), including sociolinguistic as well as linguistic features. Another possible grouping would be grammatical competence, sociolinguistic competence, discourse competence, and strategic competence, as suggested by Canale (2, p. 82). Since testing in the discourse phase involves a broad sampling of linguistic and nonlinguistic items, grading must be subjective to a great degree, that is, based on teachers' professional judgments in a more or less directive fashion.

6. *The test sequence should be incorporated into the course syllabus so that the progression of the test sequence is respected.* For example, verifications of short duration, perhaps five to ten minutes, should be used for the recognition and memory phases. Discrete-point formats are highly appropriate to the short duration of verifications; and, since discrete-point items are easy to correct, verifications can be given often. Quizzes of medium

duration, fifteen to thirty minutes, should be used to recheck certain items of the memory phase and to test the contextualized phase. Quizzes would thus consist of a few discrete-point items and mostly contextual items, such as personal questions to which a simple answer is appropriate, fill-in-the-blank paragraphs in a modified cloze format, and dehydrated sentences. Major tests of long duration, forty to sixty minutes, would recheck a few items from the contextualized phase and concentrate on items in the discourse phase, such as dialogue completion and essay writing. Major tests would thus include a combination of both contextualized items and more open-ended items in which students are required to produce substantial chunks of discourse.

7. *Teachers will want to proceed through the phases of the testing sequence at different rates and in different ways* for students at different stages of instruction. For example, for beginning students (those who would rate within the Novice Level on the OPI) most testing would be in the recognition and memory phases, working with single words or memorized material in a discrete-point format, with initial attempts into the contextualized phase. For intermediate students (those who would rate within the Intermediate Level on the OPI) discrete-point items might be used initially to recheck learned material, and then testing would concentrate on the contextualized phase, with some fairly simple items in the discourse phase. For above-average students (those who would rate at the Advanced or Superior levels on the OPI) the memorized phase could be rechecked at home using self-graded exercises or in the language laboratory using audio tapes and/or computer-assisted instruction, so that classroom time could be reserved for selective testing in the contextualized phase and especially for thorough testing in the discourse phase. Within the confines of what is appropriate to their level of ability, students would repeat the testing sequence for each topic of the course syllabus, hence the term *multi-sequence evaluation*.

Example of multi-sequence evaluation for writing

As an initial example, we will consider a traditional grammar point, generally tested in writing. Although the main focus of this chapter is on speaking, it would be useful to examine a writing sequence first. The proficiency movement, as pointed out earlier in this chapter, concerns all four skills; likewise, the notion of multi-sequence evaluation may be used in testing writing, reading, and listening, as well as speaking. However, since we traditionally teach from a structural syllabus and thus test writing, and especially grammar, more systematically than we do speaking, teachers may be able to envision the system better through a written example than through an oral one. We will then move to specific examples of multi-sequence evaluation for speaking.

Grammar point to be tested: the verb *to have*
Verification items for use in the recognition and memory phases.

Recognition
a) Which of the following sentences contains a form of the verb *to have*?
 A. Marie hears cars.
 B. Karen has chickens.
 C. Ben hates beer.
b) In the following paragraph, identify which words are forms of the verb *to have.*

 Ken and Mavis have a son named Sean who is a little demon. He has more energy than you would believe. He hits his sister Martha on the hands and head. Martha, of course, hates this and has a fit each time they get into a fight. Ken and Mavis don't know how to solve the problem. Their friends tell them Sean will outgrow it. They certainly hope so.

Memory
c) Complete the paradigm of the verb *to have.*

 I have   we_____
 you_____   you have
 he, she, it_____ they_____

d) In the following dialogue, fill in the appropriate forms of the verb *to have.*
 Linda: Hey, Peter, I _____ a new TV. It's color and _____ a 19-inch screen.
 Peter: So, big deal, my folks _____ a color TV, too, and I can watch it whenever I want.
 Linda: OK. Can we watch it tonight? Or do you_____ to study?
 Peter: I _____ already finished my homework, but we _____ to go visit my grandma. Maybe we can watch your TV tomorrow.

Items in the memory phase require little knowledge other than form. Reading may even be minimized if the student simply decides to move from blank to blank looking for the subject. In a sense, students are asked to regurgitate material, either in chart form or within a given sentence. Correction is objective and quick, in that only one answer is appropriate.

Quiz items for use in the contextualized phase.
a) Use the following elements to make complete sentences.
 I want to stay home, but Melinda / to have / to go / store / tonight / .

My term paper is due tomorrow and I haven't typed it yet.
You / to have / typewriter / ?

b) Complete the paragraph by choosing one of the verbs from the following list and putting it into the appropriate form. Pay special attention to tense.

to have   to be   to go   to want

   Yesterday, I_____ out to dinner with my friends Rhonda and Josh. We_____ to get a pizza, but Rhonda_____ on a diet so we decided to_____ to a new Chinese restaurant. I_____ not too happy about that, because I didn't _____ a lot of money. Josh always_____ a lot to eat; he_____ never happy until we've spent all my money. This time was no exception. If I_____ to go out to eat again tonight, I think I_____ by myself.

c) Write each response in a complete sentence using the verb *to have*.
   Tell me about your family.
   How many sisters do you have?
   Does your family have a house or an apartment?
   You say your brother is out of school. Does he have a job?

Items in the contextualized phase are more difficult than items in the memory phase in that students have to choose among a series of options involving different instructional points. Furthermore, since the items are contextualized, the student must understand the sentence or paragraph in order to answer and must know in which contexts the items tested should appear. Answers, however, are still straightforward and can generally be graded easily by assigning points for key parts of the answer: in (a) 1 point for each element to be used in composing the sentence; in (b) 1 point for choice and 1 point for form; in (c) 1 point for an appropriate answer, 1 point for the verb *to have* or an appropriate substitute, and 1 point for the rest of the sentence.

Major test items for use in the discourse phase.
a) Read this dialogue. Then create Elizabeth's role. Keep in mind that Elizabeth is a determined woman who likes to get her own way.

   Elizabeth and Nicholas are engaged. They have saved 10,000 dollars to spend for their honeymoon and things they need to set up a household. Sitting around the dinner table, they discuss what they should do.
   Nicholas: Well, it's clear that we should get a car first thing.
   Elizabeth: Why? I don't think_____.

Nicholas: What do you mean? Everyone needs a car. What will we do when we need to go buy groceries?
Elizabeth: _____.
Nicholas: So what do you want to do with the money?
Elizabeth: _____.
Nicholas: That's stupid.
Elizabeth: That's your opinion. I _____.

b) Complete the following statements to describe your apartment or room or one that you can imagine.

My apartment/room is _____.
On the desk I _____,
because I _____. In the corner
I like to keep _____. My
roommate _____. I don't mind
_____ so much, but I really
_____. Our life would be better if
_____.

c) Write a short description of what you and three of your friends have to do tonight. Write an introductory sentence, list and compare your activities, and end with a summary statement (50–75 words).

Items in the discourse stage are obviously so open-ended that we can only set the scene for using the grammatical point, the verb *to have,* that we are considering here. This is, in fact, the key to discourse-phase items: students respond using the full range of language available to them and are not channeled into specific responses. In this final phase, test items are more function-based than structure-based. This is, of course, highly appropriate: the early phases concern learning the tools; the final phase, putting the tools to use. Items in the discourse phase are naturally more subjective, although grading can be directed by allotting a certain number of points to each segment of the response. Points should also be given for breadth and appropriateness of vocabulary and discourse strategies, such as cohesiveness, logic, complexity, and creativity.

Advantages of multi-sequence evaluation

Multi-sequence evaluation has two prime advantages: high face validity and directive learning. In this system of testing, we are honest and straightforward about what we ask students to do: recognize features, memorize them, use them in structured contexts, or integrate them in free discourse.

As we lead students through the testing sequence, we encourage them to realize that they must first acquire linguistic building blocks and tools and then, as soon as possible, begin to use the tools to put the blocks together. Multi-sequence evaluation does not propose anything radically different in terms of items for classroom testing; in fact, it strives to relegitimatize certain test items that, for some, have ceased to be useful. More important, it opposes the all too common tendency for all verifications, quizzes, and tests to follow a similar pattern. It imposes a progressive system of classroom evaluation aimed at leading students toward greater functional proficiency.

Examples of multi-sequence evaluation for testing oral skills

We will now focus on the oral skills, particularly speaking, with some listening in the preparatory recognition phase. The need to include speaking in our achievement tests has recently received much attention, perhaps because the OPI measures speaking and because we have, as a profession, neglected testing speaking for so long. Not only do we need to give a speaking test now and then in order to show students in a practical way that we value speaking, but also we need to develop a systematic means of evaluating speaking thoroughly and progressively as we do the other skills. Multi-sequence evaluation offers a model for such systematic evaluation.

A system for evaluating speaking is perhaps best organized around functional concepts, the linguistic tasks that students are asked to perform. Through functional usage, grammar, pronunciation, vocabulary, discourse, and sociolinguistic features are put to work in effecting actual communication. Research by Kaplan suggests that students' oral work improves best if class practice is targeted at or slightly above the students' current proficiency level (Kaplan, 7). Thus, if our students are just beginning, we would want first to teach and test them on the Novice Level; when they have reached the Intermediate Level, we would concentrate our teaching and testing on Intermediate- and Advanced-Level tasks; when they have reached the Advanced Level, our focus would be on the Advanced and Superior levels. The proficiency guidelines, then, offer us an orientation for implementing multi-sequence evaluation.

In the examples that follow, we will examine the four main levels of the OPI scale (Novice, Intermediate, Advanced, and Superior) and consider the types of test items that multi-sequence evaluation would lead us to use with students at each proficiency level.

Achievement tests for students within the Novice Level of proficiency

Function: Listing
Topic: Clothes

Recognition phase
The teacher displays a series of pictures of people wearing different types of clothing. The teacher asks simple questions, such as, "Who is wearing a dress?" Students respond by pointing to the correct picture. Answers can be graded right or wrong. The number of questions asked can be quite limited, perhaps one to five. This quick verification can be done by having students come to the front of the room for a few minutes during another activity such as group work, a written exercise, or a quiz, or can be done with class members taking turns while seated. In the latter case, volunteers might get the first opportunity to answer; anyone who has not volunteered by the end of the question period would have to answer a question selected by the teacher.

In quick verifications such as this, it is highly appropriate to consider multiple testing occasions as Canale suggests: individuals are tested rather informally over a period of some length, a marking period of more than a month, for instance (Canale, 2, p. 88). Points are earned on each testing occasion, contributing to one grade for oral verification at the end of the marking period.

Memory phase
Using one of the procedures suggested above, the teacher asks students to name and identify items of clothes from the vocabulary covered, for example:

"What am I wearing?"
"Name three things you would wear on a sunny day."

Ideally, lists of clothes would be appropriate here; however, this could be combined with memorized sentence starters, such as, "You are wearing ..." and "I'd wear ...". Grading could be either right or wrong for each piece of clothing mentioned or could include 1 point for giving the vocabulary word and 1 point for pronouncing it correctly.

Contextualized phase
The teacher leads students through a familiar or memorized dialogue to focus on the key point, here the vocabulary of clothing, by indicating to students how they are to respond.

Teacher (playing the role of Mary): Hi, Ann, I've saved a bit of money. Would you like to go shopping with me? (Say yes, and indicate what you want to buy.)

Student (playing the role of Ann) responds:_____.

Teacher: OK. I need something to wear to the party Saturday night. What do you think I should get? (Suggest something.)

*Student:*_____.

Teacher: I don't think that would do. Do you have any other ideas? (Suggest something else.)

*Student:*_____.

Teacher: Great. That's what I'll look for. Let's go right away.

Such guided dialogues are suggested by Wesche (24, p. 562) based on van Ek's specifications of threshold second language objectives for European school children and adults. This exercise can be done either with the teacher working individually with students, as the example suggests, or with students working in pairs. When students work in pairs, one student is given a card with the teacher's role, to be read aloud; the other student responds. Roles can be reversed for future testing on either the same or subsequent days. Grading can be done simply by students, either advanced students who are comfortable with the material or fellow students who are supplied with a specially prepared vocabulary list to help them offer feedback to their classmates. Using student graders, of course, saves considerable instructor time as well as serving as a learning experience for the graders. However, it would probably necessitate grading on a simplified basis, such as marking each vocabulary word as acceptable or unacceptable. If a more refined grading system is desired, the teacher can grade such features as key vocabulary word (2 points), accuracy of the rest of the sentence (1 point), pronunciation/fluency (1 point), logic and discourse appropriateness (1 point). If recording facilities are available, both the teacher stimulus and student response could be taped to allow for grading at a later time.

<u>Discourse phase.</u>

This phase, of course, is not appropriate when students are limited to memorized material. First attempts might include having students act out memorized dialogues or doing simple exercises generally associated with Intermediate-Level proficiency. It is important to remember that students who are still on the Novice Level need to practice Intermediate-Level tasks in order to advance to the Intermediate Level. Therefore, students go through the testing sequence many times within each proficiency level and even, if you will, between adjacent proficiency levels. The term *multisequence evaluation* was coined to express this cyclic notion.

Achievement testing sequence for students within the Intermediate Level of proficiency

Function: Asking questions
Topic: Interrogative words and structures

Recognition phase
    The teacher or tape says a sentence of which the last part is inaudible. This can be made pseudo-authentic with sound effects such as slamming a door, having the teacher cough, as is done in an exercise of the beginning French textbook *Allons-y* (1), or putting static into the recording to simulate a poor phone connection, as suggested by Omaggio (13, p. 53). The student is to choose the appropriate question to elicit the missing information.

Cue: That's too early. I'll meet you at (interference).

    A. Where will you meet me?
    B. When will you meet me?
    C. Why will you meet me?

This test type is graded right or wrong. It can be given in the lab or orally in class to everyone at once.

Memory phase
    The teacher sets up a situation in which students can use questions they have memorized. The situation can be given to the students orally, in class or in the lab, or can be given to them written on a card which they first read aloud. The cue can be presented either in English (to avoid using target vocabulary) or in the foreign language. The students should ask a predetermined number of questions for each situation.

Cue: You are planning to go on a picnic with a friend. You want to know what the weather is like and what time the grocery store opens so you can buy food. You ask your friend.
Student: (Asks the two appropriate questions studied in class.)

A similar idea is presented by Valdman and Moody as part of the Indiana University French Communicative Ability Test (IUFCAT). They suggest grading according to four parameters: (1) pragmatic and semantic appropriateness, (2) grammatical well-formedness, (3) pronunciation accuracy and fluency, and (4) amount of information communicated—each within a limited range (0 1 2, 0 1 2 3, or 0 1 2 3 4), depending on the complexity of the required response (Valdman and Moody, 22).

Contextualized phase

The teacher makes a statement, either in class or on tape in the lab. The student asks one or more logical questions to request further information about the teacher's statement.

Cue: By the way, I met your sister last night.
Student: (Where did you meet her? Who introduced you?, etc.)

This type of test item, suggested by Howard (5, p. 282) can be administered in a variety of ways: with recorded statements in the lab, by calling students to the desk; by making the statements to the class and eliciting questions from several students for each situation; by pairing students, having one student read the statement and the other provide an oral question which the first then writes down. In the last case, grading would be possible only on content and perhaps form, but not on pronunciation. Ideally, grading might involve a range (0 1 2 3, for example) for three parameters: (1) pragmatic and semantic appropriateness, (2) grammatical well-formedness, and (3) pronunciation accuracy and fluency, such as is suggested by the IUFCAT guidelines.

Discourse phase

The teacher shows the student a set of pictures, one of which the teacher has selected to be the target picture. For example, there might be six pictures showing a couple seated at a sidewalk café, all with one slight detail different—waiter present/waiter absent; man with raised glass/man about to start eating, etc. The student asks the teacher questions in order to try to determine which picture the teacher has chosen. The teacher responds to the questions naturally, but with minimal information, so that more questions must be asked (Palmer, 14). Since this item involves interchange, it cannot be done in the lab. In addition to doing it with each student individually, the teacher can involve a group of students, giving credit to each student for the questions asked. Grading should include pragmatic and grammatical appropriateness (including perhaps the choice of questions asked, to encourage listening comprehension and logic), grammatical well-formedness, pronunciation accuracy and fluency, and perhaps, the number of questions asked. An extra point might be awarded for guessing the chosen picture.

Achievement test items for students within the Advanced Level of proficiency

Function: Narration
Topic: Expressions of future time

Recognition phase
   The teacher reads a statement or question aloud, or on tape for use in the lab. The student chooses the most natural rejoinder.

Teacher: I plan to study all weekend. How about you?

   A. I studied last weekend.
   B. I've got a test, but I hope to get out Saturday night.
   C. I go to the movies.

Administration is straightforward: responses are written and the entire class can be tested at once. Grading is, of course, one point for each correct choice.

Memory phase
   Transformation. The teacher makes a statement in the past tense about something he or she has done. Students respond by saying when in the future they will do the same thing.

Cue: I went to the movies last weekend.
Student: I'm going to the movies this weekend.

This item can, of course, be done in class or in the lab. It can be expanded by asking for several different ways to express the notion of future time ("I'll go . . . ," "I hope to go . . . ," "I plan to go . . ."); different students in the class can provide different possibilities in a group-testing situation. Grading should consider situational appropriateness of the response (including use of an appropriate future time indicator), grammaticalness, and pronunciation and fluency.

Contextualized phase
   Description/narration. The teacher provides a drawing showing a series of events. Future time is indicated by having a date, calendar, or clock on the frame of the drawing. Students tell a story based on the drawing. This can be done by individual students in class or in the lab, or as a group/class effort with each individual contributing a different part. If done as a group effort, the students should be required to tell the story in order, so that a complete, logical narration/description results.

Telling stories from pictures is a common testing technique used, for instance, on the MLA, Advanced Placement, and Ilyin Oral Proficiency examinations. Grading should consider semantic appropriateness, grammaticalness (both of the future form and of other elements), pronunciation and fluency, and discourse logic.

Discourse phase
    Pair/group discussion. Two to four students are given seven to twelve minutes to discuss a topic such as "What will the world be like in fifty years? Describe, for example, the cities, the interests and occupations of people, technology, the environment," or "What will the life of your granddaughter be like? Consider her family, her job, her manner of dress, her hobbies, her fears, her dreams." The teacher either listens and grades on the spot or participates in the discussion, recording it for grading later. Another option is for two teachers or an advanced student and a teacher to work together, one to participate in the discussion and one to grade. Grading should include semantic appropriateness, grammaticalness, breadth of vocabulary, pronunciation and accuracy, discourse features, and risk-taking. If teacher grading time is at a premium, students could be asked to write down the points that their group discussed. A quick oral check would be to ask each group or individual, depending on time available, to state one point. Grading would then be based on the one oral statement and the written list.

As Canale points out, group tests in which several people are tested at once are quite practical for testing speaking skills of a large number of students. Two potentially problematic variables to keep in mind, however, are variations in group dynamics and in the observer's ability to assess reliably several people at the same time (Canale, 2, p. 87).

Achievement tests for students within the Superior Level of proficiency

Function: Supporting an opinion
Topic: TV and the press

Recognition phase
    The teacher reads a series of opinion statements about TV and the press. Students indicate whether the speaker is pro or con these forms of media.
1) It is clear that television is a detriment to our society.
2) The press has theoretically a vital social role; however, practically it is little more than a vehicle for charlatans such as gossip columnists.

3) In the final analysis, I hesitate to say anything positive about the role of either television or the press in modern society.

Memory phase

Oral cloze. The teacher reads once or twice a familiar or memorized passage with words missing. The deleted words may be either determined systematically, such as every nth word as in the traditional cloze test, or selected by the teacher for the potential they offer as interesting and appropriate test items, as is often done in modified classroom cloze. In order to focus on a key topic, such as supporting opinion in this case, the modified procedure might be preferable. In this example, for instance, key items used in making and supporting opinion statements could be deleted, including appropriate verb tenses, emotionally charged adjectives and adverbs that reveal the opinion of the narrator, and expressions of argumentation such as "in my (opinion)" and "on the (other hand)." Students use hypothesizing techniques and memory recall of the passage to supply the missing words either orally or on paper.

Writing is obviously more efficient, yet, as Oller points out, students might become progressively lost without continued feedback on the appropriateness of the answers they are giving. Oral answers would allow immediate feedback and thus minimize this problem (Oller, 11, p. 3). Grading can be done on either an exact word basis or by giving credit for any word that is semantically appropriate and grammatically correct, perhaps with one-half point for each. If the latter option is chosen, the exercise type may belong more rightly in the contextual phase.

Example:

We are clearly a television generation. We have only to examine a few (examples) to see the gravity of our situation. Parents plan the daily routine of their preschoolers around the (sacred) teacher, "Sesame Street." What is (worse), adolescents spend their evenings watching MTV. Even more (symptomatic), perhaps, adults spend millions of dollars a year nationally on cable networks and Beta Max recorders (so) as not to miss their favorite show. In my (opinion), this situation is extremely dangerous. Television, we (might) contend, is a chief reason for the breakdown of the nuclear family, for noncommunication among adults, and for a decline in the creativity of our youth. (If) we were to extend this trend twenty years forward, we (would) see a generation of television addicts, zombies in front of the large screen tube. This (alarming) situation clearly calls for remedial action. I (challenge) you to confront this (issue) and to respond to it with force.

Contextualized phase

Half dialogue. The teacher gives students a dialogue with only one part written in. Students would not be shown the dialogue in advance; however, the topic (the media) or the functions required (showing disapproval) might be announced. Students have a few minutes to think about how they would create the missing half of the dialogue. The dialogue is then role-played spontaneously.

This activity, suggested by Howard (5, p. 283), demands active participation of both the teacher and student. Depending on the classroom situation, the teacher's role could be delegated to an advanced student, a native assistant, a visitor invited to the class for this purpose, or another student in the same class. In the last case, roles could be exchanged in subsequent testings. Grading should include effective communication of functions, semantic and discourse appropriateness, grammaticalness, breadth of vocabulary, pronunciation and fluency, and creativity or risk-taking. The activity could be graded either globally or by individual responses in the dialogue. If two students are used, the one who reads might receive points for pronunciation, intonation, and fluency.

Teacher: So, what do you think of our school paper? I'm the new advisor and I really want to know.
*Student:*_____.
Teacher: What makes you say that?
*Student:*_____.
Teacher: I don't understand. Can you give me a precise example?
*Student:*_____.
Teacher: Would that really work?
*Student:*_____.
Teacher: I see what you mean. Thanks for the advice. Why don't you sign up to work with me? We'd make quite a team.

Discourse phase

Topic cards. As part of the oral testing procedure in fourth-semester Spanish at the University of Illinois, teachers prepare a series of topic cards on announced topics covered in class. The cards include a statement of the issue and several questions that the student might want to address in making an opinion statement. Students draw a card and give an impromptu monologue on the topic. After the monologue, the instructor asks questions to which the student responds.

Topic: Methods of Communication: Television and the Press. You may wish to include the following in your monologue:
As forms of communication, what are the advantages and disadvantages of television and newspapers?

What, if any, are the various effects of television on children?
Should TV and the press always reflect reality?
What are your feelings with regard to advertising in newspapers and on TV?

Examples of follow-up questions include: What are some negative effects that television can cause among adults? What is your favorite program? Why do you like it?

The monologue and follow-up questions are graded separately as follows:

Monologue

Fluency	1 2 3 4 5 6
Vocabulary	1 2 3 4 5 6 7 8
Structure	1 2 3 4 5 6
Comprehensibility	1 2 3 4 5 6 7 8 9 10 11 12 13 14

Answering questions on monologue

Fluency	1 2 3 4 5
Vocabulary	1 2 3
Structure	1 2 3 4
Comprehensibility	1 2 3 4 5 6 7 8
Listening Comp.	1 2 3 4 5 6

Each scale corresponds to a description, such as the following for the six points allotted to structure of the monologue:
1 No utterances structurally correct
2 Very few utterances structurally correct
3 Some utterances rendered correctly, but major structural problems remain
4 Many correct utterances, but with definite structural problems
5 Most utterances rendered correctly, with some minor structural errors
6 Utterances almost always correct
[Developed by Boylan, reported in Omaggio, 13, pp. 62–69.]

These are examples of incorporating a progression of oral testing into the typical, busy classroom. Teachers will have to be flexible, of course, in adapting these ideas to fit their particular circumstances. In devising a grading system, there are three important concepts. First, speaking tests do not have to be graded as precisely as written grammar tests; in fact, since speaking is ideally a highly personal activity, subjective grading is often more appropriate. Snyder suggests two main orientations for grading oral tests: idea-based, in which the grade reflects mainly the amount and type of information communicated; and quality-based, in which the grade reflects the accuracy and complexity of the speech (Snyder, 18, p. 37). Ideally, both should be measured, but it is better to measure only one of the two at any specific time than not to measure speaking at all for fear of complex and time-consuming grading. Second, if oral skills are tested systematically, such as through the multi-sequence evaluation system suggested here, no one test need be overly demanding, on either the student or the teacher. Third, the bottom line is that responsible feedback on speaking is more important than the objectivity of any one grade.

Achievement interview

In order to prepare our students for functional use of the foreign language in the foreign culture, we need to do systematic evaluation of oral skills throughout our courses. Especially if one of our goals is to prepare students to perform well on the OPI, we might want to add a final, cumulative step to our multi-sequence evaluation process: an achievement interview.

The purpose of an achievement interview is to give students experience in an extended one-on-one conversation and in some of the tasks used in the OPI, while staying within the course framework. This takes some of the fear of the unknown out of the OPI and, more important, demonstrates to students what they do and do not know. Students are often delighted with the success they feel in communicating completely in the foreign language for five to fifteen minutes and are even eager to fill in the gaps that they themselves recognize in their language as a result of this conversation. A positive student response to the oral interview was, in fact, found in research by Shohamy, who compared attitudes toward the oral interview of the Foreign Service Institute, on which the ACTFL/ETS interview is based, with attitudes toward cloze tests; on a scale from 1 to 5, with 5 being high, the oral interview rated 4.0 and the cloze test, 3.24 (Shohamy, 17). Few would disagree that positive student attitudes are helpful if not crucial to classroom learning. Oral interviews, given both as part of an achievement testing battery in the classroom and as a proficiency test, can thus motivate learning.

As two final examples in this chapter, we will look briefly at two models of achievement interviews currently being developed at the University of Wisconsin-Madison. The first has been used in the second-semester French course, administered twice a semester; the second, in a third-semester French course, administered once a semester. Both are designed for large-scale use, to be administered by teaching assistants and faculty.

Single-student achievement interview. Students make appointments to be interviewed by their instructor outside of class. One class day and some office hours are cancelled to allow time for interviewing. Students are told that the interview will consist of two parts: reading of a distributed text that they can practice in the lab and an impromptu conversation. The reading is done first, as a warm-up and nerve-settler for the interview, and counts 15 percent of the test grade; the conversation is the main part of the test, counting 85 percent. To prepare for the impromptu conversation, students are given three vocabulary areas and a few grammar points (mainly verb tenses and interrogative forms) to review from among the material covered. There is nothing to memorize nor are there questions to prepare in advance. Instructors receive a sample list of open-ended topic questions, such as: "What do you plan to do this summer?" "Tell me about your roommate: what does he or she look like? What does he or she like to do?" "Ask me about my hobbies." These serve only as examples; the actual interview questions are devised during the interview, based on the responses of the student. The only requirement of the interview is that it measure key features represented on the grading grid. As this particular achievement interview is geared toward the Intermediate and Advanced levels of the OPI, students are asked to describe and narrate in present, past, and future times and to ask questions. Each interview takes approximately seven minutes.

Grading is done on the grading grid represented in Table 1, either on the spot, if the instructor feels comfortable, or from a recording. Grading is done globally within categories; individual errors are not counted. As the numbers in the grid indicate, categories are weighted so that grammar, including use and accuracy of associated functions counts 33 percent; breadth of content, or vocabulary, 25 percent; discourse features, including comprehension and communicative ability, 17 percent; and pronunciation, 10 percent. The grammar category receives the most weight since use and accuracy of the functions of describing, narrating, and asking questions are measured here. Vocabulary follows, measured both for breadth and accuracy. Discourse elements receive less weight, only because they are difficult to measure in this limited format and because more emphasis seems to inflate grades. Pronunciation receives the least emphasis since it is also measured by the oral reading warm-up. The total is 85 percent; and the additional 15 percent is reserved for the oral reading. This grid is designed both for the purposes of grading and to provide feedback to students on areas of strength and weakness.

Paired-student achievement interview. In the paired-student model there is no warm-up reading for pronunciation, although one could be added. Students are given instructions that are very similar to those of the single-student interview, except that students sign up with a partner and expect to be speaking mainly with that partner, rather than with the teacher. The

Table 1. Grading Grid for French Achievement Interview

	A+	A	AB	B	BC	C	D	F		
I. Grammar (33%)										
A. Verbs										
1. Ability to talk in the present tense	50	47	45	43	40	37	33	28	15	8
2. Ability to talk about the past	50	47	45	43	40	37	33	28	15	8
3. Ability to talk about the future (*futur proche; avoir envie de* + inf., *vouloir* + inf., *avoir l'intention de, compter* + inf., *conditionnel,* etc.)	50	47	45	43	40	37	33	28	15	8
B. Nouns and noun phrases (articles, adjectives, agreements, etc.)	60	56	54	52	48	44	39	33	18	9
C. Interrogatives	60	56	54	52	48	44	39	33	18	9
D. General syntax not covered above (including adverbs, conjunctions, object pronouns, prepositions)	60	56	54	52	48	44	39	33	18	9
II. Pronunciation (10%)										
A. Individual sounds	50	47	45	43	40	37	33	28	15	8
B. Intonation, rhythm, conversational flow	50	47	45	43	40	37	33	28	15	8
III. Vocabulary and topics used (25%) (breadth of vocabulary used appropriately)	250	235	225	215	200	185	163	138	75	38
IV. Discourse (17%)										
A. Comprehension, appropriateness of response	90	85	81	77	72	67	59	50	27	14
B. Information communicated	80	75	72	69	64	59	52	44	24	12

Interview Total: _____ /850

Plus Reading Total: _____ /150

Percentage: _____ /1000

Grade: _____

interview begins with the teacher asking the first student a question eliciting narration in the future (for example, "What are you going to do this summer?"). After the first student answers, the second student asks the first student questions about what he said. The roles are then reversed for a similar question testing the same function. The teacher then asks for a narration in the past through a question such as, "What did you do last summer?" Again each student answers at some length and partners ask each other questions. The third segment of the interview is a role play in which both students and the teacher play a part. The role plays are given to students in advance with the understanding that they can look up key vocabulary and think about the situation, but that they cannot write out and memorize a dialogue, since the teacher will be playing an unannounced role. Grading is also done on the grid in Table 1, except that points for an oral reading are not included. A paired-student interview takes about fifteen minutes.

The single-student interview has the advantage of having each student talk with the "perfect" model, the teacher, thereby avoiding the problem of pairing students of different ability. The paired interview has the advantages of "security in numbers"; of promoting a less tense and perhaps more natural conversation; and of the high motivation for partners to get together and practice. Since students realize that they cannot practice the actual questions to be used, they create questions to practice the functions and topics, in order to gain facility and confidence. Teacher time is about the same (seven minutes for one student or fifteen minutes for two); however, correction time may be greater in the two-student model if the difficulty in evaluating two students at once makes grading on the spot too difficult, thereby necessitating grading from tapes.

Both of these achievement interviews are used as major parts of the course grade at the University of Wisconsin-Madison. This is appropriate since they are limited to topics and grammar points covered in the course. Grading, as indicated on the grid, is based on teacher expectations for students at that level. This, of course, is very different from expectations for proficiency. This difference in expectation is crucial: according to preliminary testing at UW-Madison, students in second- and third-semester French are probably mostly in the Novice and Intermediate ranges in oral proficiency. They perform Advanced-Level tasks such as narrating and describing in the past and future only in a very limited and inconsistent manner. However, in achievement testing we can measure and evaluate these initial attempts fairly, as long as grading follows course expectations and not the OPI rating scale. It is, of course, highly inappropriate to convert OPI ratings into course grades. The achievement interview helps avoid this tendency; in form and function it reflects the OPI, but in grading it is substantially different.

Conclusion

This chapter brings three messages to the classroom teacher. The first is a message of reassurance: it is indeed appropriate to teach to the OPI when a main goal of the course is functional use of the foreign language, and discrete-point test formats, such as multiple-choice and fill-in-the-blank, which might be considered by some to have outlived their usefulness, are still viable forms for testing toward communicative objectives when incorporated into a testing sequence that leads toward functional language use. The second is a message of motivation and encouragement: to test speaking regularly and to organize testing of all four skills in a way that will lead students more directly from learning isolated linguistic items to applying this knowledge in real-world communication.

As a means of organizing testing toward this end, multi-sequence evaluation is proposed as a testing progression, to be used cyclically throughout classroom learning. It is hoped that the specific test items offered as examples of multi-sequence evaluation are precise enough to stimulate teacher creativity, yet loose enough to encourage flexibility; for they will work only when shaped to the pedagogical goals of the teacher, the expressed needs of the students, and the practical demands of the instructional situation.

Finally, this chapter suggests a third message: the implied impact of oral proficiency and achievement testing on the curriculum, on the daily teaching of our classes. If we test what we teach, we also teach what we test. If we then incorporate multi-sequence evaluation into our instructional programs, we will most likely incorporate the phases of recognition, memory, contextualization, and discourse into our teaching. If we teach to the OPI, tasks such as role-playing, question-asking, narrating, describing, explaining, and comparing will become integral parts of our lesson plans, as we reshape our curricula to include more proficiency-based activities. In order to make the time for these communicative tasks, we may begin, as Nerenz and Knop (10) urge, to restructure classroom interactions to include less teacher talk and more student pair and group work, in order to give students more individual opportunities to practice speaking, and to consider eagerly innovations such as computer-assisted instruction that offer tutorials for memorization of vocabulary and simple manipulations of grammar, which ultimately should liberate precious class time for the more personal interaction essential to meaningful conversation. Using class time efficiently to help students acquire functional linguistic skills is, after all, the most promising outcome of proficiency—more effective teaching.

References, From Achievement toward Proficiency through Multi-Sequence Evaluation

1. Bragger, Jeannette D., and Donald B. Rice. *Allons-y!*. Boston: Heinle & Heinle, 1984.
2. Canale, Michael. "Testing in a Communicative Approach," pp. 79–92 in Gilbert A. Jarvis, ed., *The Challenge for Excellence in Foreign Language Education.* Middlebury, VT: Northeast Conference, 1984.
3. Clark, John L. D. "Language Testing: Past and Current Status—Directions for the Future." *The Modern Language Journal* 67 (1983):431–43.
4. Freed, Barbara. Information given in "POPT Newsletter," University of New Hampshire, March 1984. See also Barbara Freed, "Establishing Proficiency-Based Language Requirements." *ADFL Bulletin* 13 (1982):6–12.
5. Howard, Françoise. "Testing Communicative Proficiency in French as a Second Language: A Search for Procedures." *The Canadian Modern Language Journal* 36 (1980):272–89.
6. Jiménez, Reynaldo, and Carol J. Murphy. "Proficiency Projects in Action," pp. 201–17 in Theodore V. Higgs, ed., *Teaching for Proficiency, the Organizing Principle.* The ACTFL Foreign Language Education Series, vol. 15. Lincolnwood, IL: National Textbook Co., 1984.
7. Kaplan, Isabelle. "Oral Proficiency Testing and the Language Curriculum: Two Experiments in Curricular Design for Conversation Courses." *Foreign Language Annals,* in press.
8. Liskin-Gasparro, Judith E. "The ACTFL Proficiency Guidelines: A Historical Perspective," pp. 11–42 in Theodore V. Higgs, ed., *Teaching for Proficiency, the Organizing Principle.* The ACTFL Foreign Language Education Series, vol. 15. Lincolnwood, IL: National Textbook Co., 1984.
9. Nerenz, Anne G. "Utilizing Class Time in Foreign Language Instruction," pp. 78–89 in D. P. Benseler, ed., *Teaching the Basics in the Foreign Language Classroom.* Proceedings of the Central States Conference on Foreign Language Teaching. Lincolnwood, IL: National Textbook Co., 1978.
10. _____, and Constance K. Knop. "The Effects of Group Size on Students' Opportunity to Learn in the Second Language Classroom," pp. 47–60 in Alan Garfinkel, ed., *ESL and the Foreign Language Teacher.* Lincolnwood, IL: National Textbook Co., 1982.
11. Oller, John W., Jr. *Language Tests at School.* New York: Longman, 1979.
12. _____. "Language Testing Research (1979–1980)," pp. 124–50 in Robert B. Kaplan, ed., *Annual Review of Applied Linguistics.* Rowley, MA: Newbury House, 1981.
13. Omaggio, Alice. *Proficiency-Oriented Classroom Testing.* Washington, DC: Center for Applied Linguistics, 1983.
14. Palmer, A. S. "Testing Communication." *International Review of Applied Linguistics* 10 (1972):35–45.
15. Paulston, Christina Bratt. "Structural Pattern Drills: A Classification." *Foreign Language Annals* 4 (1970):187–93.
16. Postovsky, Valerian. "Effects of Delay in Oral Practice at the Beginning of Second Language Learning." *The Modern Language Journal* 58 (1971):229–39.
17. Shohamy, Elana. "Interrater and Intrarater Reliability of the Oral Interview and Concurrent Validity with Cloze Procedure in Hebrew," pp. 229–36 in John W. Oller, Jr., ed., *Issues in Language Testing Research.* Rowley, MA: Newbury House, 1983.
18. Snyder, Barbara. "Creative and Communicative Achievement Testing," pp. 34–50 in Patricia B. Westphal, ed., *Strategies for Foreign Language Teaching.*

Report of the Central States Conference on Foreign Language Teaching. Lincolnwood, IL: National Textbook Co., 1984.
19. Spolsky, Bernard. "Linguistics and Language Testers," pp. v–x in Bernard Spolsky, ed., *Approaches to Language Testing (Advances in Language Testing: Series 2)*. Arlington, VA: Center for Applied Linguistics, 1978.
20. Terrell, Tracy. "A Natural Approach to Second Language Acquisition and Learning." *The Modern Language Journal* 61 (1977):325–37.
21. Valdman, Albert. "Toward a Modified Structural Syllabus." *Studies in Second Language Acquisition* 5 (1982):34–51.
22. ———, and Marvin Moody. "Testing Communicative Ability." *The French Review* 52 (1979):552–61.
23. Valette, Rebecca M., and Renée Disick. *Modern Language Performance Objectives and Individualization: A Handbook*. New York: Harcourt Brace Jovanovich, 1972.
24. Wesche, Marjorie Bingham. "Communicative Testing in a Second Language." *The Canadian Modern Language Journal* 37 (1981):551–71.

5

Proficiency Applications beyond the Academic Classroom

Kathryn Buck
Buck Language Services

Gregory Forsythe
American Hoechst Corporation

The Field of Vision: The World "Outside" _____

This chapter offers a discussion of the world of language instruction outside the academic context. It will not try to convince the reader this world exists; this has been done. It will, instead, present a view of *what* this "outside world" needs and *how* it needs it. Although much of what will be stated here is generally applicable to an adult learning context, the

Kathryn Buck (Ph.D., University of Washington) is an independent consultant specializing in language and cultural training services for business and industry. She left university teaching in 1978 to become the first Director of Language Programs for the Carl Duisberg Society (New York), where she designed a series of corporate language and cultural training programs, instituted the Society's annual Special Seminar for Teachers of Business German, and was coeditor of the CDS publication *Teaching Business and Technical German: Problems and Prospects* (1981). She became involved in the proficiency projects in 1981 and her training includes a two-week workshop at the Defense Language Institute in Monterey, California. She assists in training oral proficiency interviewer-raters, and is coauthor, with Pardee Lowe, Jr., of provisional language performance criteria for business and industry.

Gregory Forsythe (Ph.D., University of Michigan) is Director of Human Resource Development for American Hoechst Corporation in Somerville, New Jersey, the largest foreign subsidiary of Hoechst Aktiengesellschaft (Frankfurt). He left college teaching in 1973 for a career in management and organization development. At General Motors Overseas Operations headquarters, he administered foreign language training and worked on intercultural communications training and team-building projects. Prior to joining Hoechst in 1979, he was corporate manager of management development for General Cable Corporation. He has lived and worked in the Federal Republic of Germany.

primary focus of the essay will be the history and nature of an in-house language and cultural training program in industry. The ACTFL/ETS Proficiency Projects and resulting guidelines are the catalysts, integrated with concepts of adult education, enabling the design and implementation of a comprehensive adult language instruction system, with implications of interest to the entire foreign language teaching profession (1).

Who, what, and where is "outside"?

For decades language instruction and learning in the United States was restricted mainly to "higher education" in the liberal arts or the natural sciences. In the classical tradition, this education was defined by educators to include the learning or knowledge of a foreign language, generally understood as the ability to read/translate. But *how well?* In 1957, the year of *Sputnik,* this teaching-learning endeavor assumed a markedly different cast, and the rationale for foreign language study began to mean the ability to speak, rather than primarily the ability to read/translate. But speak *how well?* By 1976, an awareness of specific career or "vocational" instruction needs within the educational process was emerging. A national survey of innovative foreign language curricula in U.S. colleges and universities revealed that a wider range of foreign language courses was becoming available (4). An awareness was also emerging that foreign language skills constitute career preparation for medical, legal, social service, and law enforcement fields, for business and industry, even for vocal music, especially opera.

Perhaps no less significant than the year of *Sputnik* in the minds of foreign language educators, and hardly less so in the mind of the general public, was 1977, the year of President Carter's stand-in interpreter for Polish. It is rumored that the interpreter was unfairly called upon to perform linguistic tasks beyond his training and experience, but the universally embarrassing results showed a worldwide public, the least concerned of whom may well have been the *American* public, that in addition to an alleged "missile gap," there was also a "language skills gap."

Now, in 1984, this dawning awareness in the academic sector has been translated into expanded course and program offerings, sometimes—especially in subject areas pertaining to business and industry—including internships. Conferences addressing such "special topics" curricula are held annually, training seminars have been instituted to prepare language professionals for these new tasks, and the initial dearth of appropriate instructional materials is yielding to more germane offerings from publishers.

Despite impetus generated by sheer survival instinct during the "Great Enrollments Depression" of the late Sixties and early Seventies, these adaptive efforts have also been well intended and well placed, clearing the way for experimentation and innovation. There are in fact real and significant language needs in the world beyond academic classrooms, needs for which it is both appropriate and possible to prepare the student.

Increasingly, articles in professional journals have documented the existence of the world "outside," and they have reported and encouraged these curriculum innovations. In addition to the professional literature, awareness has been bolstered by efforts of The President's Commission, numerous task forces, and publication of *The Tongue-Tied American,* written by one of the major proponents of foreign language study in the U.S., Congressman Paul Simon (12).

We do not propose yet another attempt to convince the reader of the *existence* of a world "outside" but rather to discuss the *nature* and *needs* of that world. It is time to look more closely at those learners beyond the academic community—especially those in medical and social services, business and industry, and other career areas—who many of yesterday's and today's students have been and will become. It is time to consider *what* they require and *how* they require it. Much of what will be stated here applies to the majority of the adult language-learning population, because they are adults and because they have a demonstrated need or desire for foreign language skills. In this respect, the university-sponsored adult or continuing education class may represent de facto the academic community's closest encounter with proficiency-focused adult education.

Achievement versus proficiency

The outside world is composed primarily of adults. A critical implication of this feature is that adults, who are mature members of the human species with many commitments and responsibilities, tend not to think in terms of achievement when assessing their needs and the tools which will help them meet those needs but in terms of capability. They ask themselves not "what have I *learned?*" but "what can I *do* now?" In not asking themselves "what do (did) I know about German/French/Russian/Spanish/Italian, etc. grammar and syntax?" but "can I read, listen to and understand, say, or write what I need/want to?" Their functional task orientation is clear. Adults are usually not in language instruction programs because an advisor recommends it as useful, a major curriculum prescribes it as necessary, or an institution requires it for admission or graduation. An adult is usually in a language instruction program because of a desire or self-perceived need for specific skills. It is not the pressure of a grade or credit hours but rather of current or anticipated *situational performance* which is operative. And although learning foreign language skills at the initial levels must necessarily be equated with achievement, true *proficiency,* as formulated by Lowe and Clifford (3), involves *functional evidence of internalized strategies for creativity.*

Yet many adults regard foreign language instruction as something which they have experienced but which has not "worked," because they cannot "do" anything. They cannot speak, read, comprehend, or write the language. Such personal anecdotal accounts usually begin with "I took it, but. . . ." Thus adults have often come to regard "languages" as something for which they have "no aptitude" or "no ear." This perception is problematic because former students erroneously mix the proverbial oranges and apples: the *actual* and the *perceived* goals of the instructional program in which they are involved. The confusion was probably not limited to the students. It is often necessary to explain to them that their "failure" and "lack of aptitude" may well have been due to confusion in the stated and unstated objectives of teachers, students, and administrators about what was being taught, why, and to what end, than to any particular aptitude or lack of it on their part. If they were being taught with a predominantly grammar/translation approach, they *were not being taught to speak,* and if their uncorrected expectation was that they were in fact being taught to speak and really couldn't do so then or cannot now, it is less a failure on their part than on the part of the "language teaching system" to clarify its objectives and educate the student to realistic expectations about what the acquisition and maintenance of various forms of proficiency involve. Learners and teachers alike have lacked realistic guidelines for defining and measuring fluency levels and the time and effort required to achieve them.

In the outside world itself, no particular dearth of opportunities to "learn" a foreign language exists: in college- and university-sponsored continuing education courses; in commercial language schools; and by means of the myriad self-study books, records, tapes, and home computer programs offered to the public by a growing number of media.

Unlike many of their college and university cousins, language schools and vendors of self-study instructional materials recognize the *functional, task-oriented* interest of the adult consumer, and they talk a language of fluency rather than of academic necessity or personal improvement per se. Their "course descriptions" are found in "catalogs" gracing every airline seat, newsstand, and mailbox.

But typically in promising far more than can realistically be achieved, they may do as much harm as good. Offered colorful palettes of languages from Afrikaans to Welsh, the reader is invited to learn a language in a few months' time, enabling him or her to feel at home in the respective countries and to never miss the meaning of conversations or be at a loss for words (ACTFL Superior and ILR 3–5!). The methods are touted as being easy, painless, and convenient. Such a course is what one needs to start speaking like a native. Success is measured by the millions of Method X graduates who now speak the new language fluently.

Common, too, is the claim that the products are complete and professional language programs, utilizing expert tutors. The learner is to be led from basic to advanced (speaking) proficiency in a basic self-study course taking only a few months and with fewer than ten hours of recorded materials. Self-study enrollments are encouraged by such diverse support features as businesslike briefcase packaging, free cassette players, and rotary verb finders.

Thus from another quarter, from other language trainers, confusion is created about what language learning involves and what fluency is. We may deserve it; it's a hard-sell, quick-fix, thoroughly American approach. Advertising power, the lack of realistic alternatives, and a market of inexperienced consumers sell these programs by the tens of thousands, even or perhaps especially in a country which has never been known for its *Sprachenfreundlichkeit.*

A third group from which confusion originates is the learners themselves. To them, a person meriting the accolade "fluent," usually in hushed tones of admiration and wonder, is anyone who can muster more sounds reminiscent of a given language faster and look more at ease doing so than they themselves can.

A fourth group, the "outside-world" employment market, operates with a set of proficiency-related criteria in mind. But it is a set for which there are virtually no definitions. In a presentation for the 1983 Eastern Michigan University Conference on Foreign Languages for Business and Industry (6), descriptive language such as this was quoted as typical of the majority of job advertisements for positions in which some level of foreign language skill is required: "Applicant should be *fluent* in one or more of the following languages." "Must be *fully bilingual.*" "*Knowledge* of Portuguese preferred." "*Excellent skills* in both German/English are necessary." "*Working knowledge* of Arabic/Hebrew required." [Emphasis ours.]

Terms such as *fluent, fully bilingual, knowledge, working knowledge, excellent skills,* and the like are not based on any system of analysis and description. It would be surprising if the business, social service, or other outside community had a system for describing its foreign language proficiency needs when foreign language professionals themselves have found it difficult to construct and articulate such a system.

Yet the "outside" does have something to offer foreign language professionals attempting to define and measure proficiency: the highly task-oriented, functional approach it takes when asked to define needs, e.g., what an employee should be able *to do.* Types of activities (functions) and types of situations (content) emerge from discussions with employees and management encouraged to help define what constitutes the employee's and the company's needs for foreign language skills. The third partner in the Functional Trisection, *accuracy,* is often more elusive but sometimes evident: "*X* needs to be able to get the general gist of the meeting." Generally, a precise response is difficult to elicit.

The inside of the outside

Recognizing the task or functional orientation of the outside community brings us one step closer to an "insider's" understanding of these groups and their needs. Further differentiating the "outside" from an academic context is the *immediacy* of the need: skills are frequently needed *now.* Only in the most progressive, enlightened circumstances is management able to see that adequate preparation of an employee with little or no prior knowledge of a given second language can require a minimum period measured in *years* if the employee is not to be virtually released from the job for intensive language study for a number of months, probably the better part of a year. This corresponds to at least one government model for intensive training, in which language learning literally *becomes* the employee's job, a luxury nongovernment contexts can seldom justify or afford. Even in extreme instances, for example, when transfer abroad is imminent, such full-time training is seldom offered for more than a month or two, at which time the employee is expected to function as a working adult in a different language and culture.

Our academic-based language training has too often failed to produce graduates, especially nonmajors, with measurable functional foreign language skills. It thus comes as no surprise that training needs beyond the academic classroom are defined by a set of paradoxical boundaries: (a) the need for long-term, frequently *from-the-bottom-up* instruction and (b) the need for immediately applicable skills.

This mandates an approach effective for both long-term instruction and immediately applicable skills. Failure to address these two needs simultaneously bodes ill for success. A third crucial factor enters into the instructional equation: one must plan and act with the awareness of *dealing with adults.* As adults, they have not only a priority nonlanguage job to perform but also a full load of other commitments typifying adult life, *each of which may take precedence over the need and desire to learn another language.* Despite the need for ongoing, long-term instruction and the pressure for immediately applicable skills, the language-learning endeavor can be given only limited priority.

To attempt this task at all, program and instructional design must address these and other substantive issues at the outset. Failure to do so will mean that instruction will fail to meet the need. Traditional models, we believe, typify this problem. These models assume three major forms: (1) college- or university-sponsored adult education courses; (2) commercial language school courses; and (3) evening instruction sponsored by a company at its own location, usually conducted by personnel from one of the above.

For all three traditional sources of instruction, the following rule applies: the farther removed the instruction from the workplace physically, the farther it is likely to be removed from the workplace conceptually. A corollary also holds: the farther instruction is removed from the work-place conceptually, the less the motivation to attend and learn. To the extent a program of instruction is designed and offered for a general adult audience, it is removed from the individual workplace and job need. Even courses offered at the workplace have often failed to teach applicable skills: they have merely shifted the location of instruction. Such a shift is often more convenient for the participants, but significant and rapid attrition rates in these courses indicate clearly that convenience does not suffice.

A program attempting to meet these needs head-on must be company- and participant-oriented, have a clear sense of specific needs, be designed for the company and the participants, be scheduled primarily for their convenience, and teach and work with them in the contexts of their daily jobs. In short, it will be a full-time, in-house endeavor.

The *ACTFL Provisional Proficiency Guidelines* (1) offer a critically important contribution to language and cultural training efforts in this context. The following pages present one such on-site program, its history, implementation of proficiency and related criteria, relationship to management development efforts, and potential ramifications of this experience for the foreign language teaching community.

The Focus: A Program Model

Background

American Hoechst Corporation (AHC), the U.S. subsidiary of Hoechst Aktiengesellschaft, Frankfurt, Federal Republic of Germany, began planning a new, company-tailored on-site second language skills training program in the summer of 1978. Since 1978 the company has provided German language courses taught by a commercial language school. The courses meet in the evenings, once a week per class, and are open to all employees and their spouses. Instruction is not necessarily linked to job content, nor has there been a formal attempt to measure results.

Nonetheless there was a perceived need to teach employees the language skills demanded by their jobs, and with the implementation of the new program in 1979, an attempt was made to tie instruction and use of skills directly to job needs. Familiar with programs offered to companies by commercial language schools, the authors had come to believe that instruction done in-house, as part of the workday, and training for functions, contexts, and levels of accuracy as actually dictated by the job would meet the organization's and the individual's needs better than outside sources could. In addition, the instructional forum could be utilized to help overcome some frequent culture-based misunderstandings common to multicultural situations.

To ensure relevance to the job and therefore motivation, teaching materials would include working documents from the trainees' jobs, focusing on "live company jargon," general business vocabulary, and the more specific vocabulary of the international chemical/pharmaceutical industry. The instructor would consciously manage the classroom learning process to engender commitment and *esprit*. Extensive individual tutoring would ensure continued *in vivo* assessment of needs and refinement of skills.

In the five years since 1979, enrollment has increased to four times the level of the pilot program. Enrollments increased even in 1982, a year of budget reductions, layoffs, early retirements, and general belt-tightening. In 1984 the program has continued its large enrollment and a second instructor has been engaged. An understanding of the program's funding offers further testimony to its success: each trainee must obtain his or her manager's agreement to assume the annual costs, which measured per instructional hour are far less than commercial rates but as a percentage of a manager's training budget can be substantial, sometimes accounting for all of the manager's training dollars in one year. To date, there have been very few objections to the cost.

Now, five years into the experiment, the program could be termed secure and successful, needing only further refinements of a successfully applied, initial instructional system. Yet there are improvements we feel it is critical to make if the program is to maintain and increase its effectiveness. The proficiency guidelines can assist us in meeting challenges involved in providing language training outside an academic context, in a professional, adult environment where a clear need for skills exists but where the acquisition of these skills can rarely be given a high priority.

The program is managed from the Human Resources Development function of the corporate Department of Human Resources. Management development efforts typically encounter their share of motivational challenges. The AHC German program faces four main challenges, each of which represents an inextricable mix of individual motivation and organizational systemic problems: (1) absenteeism: businesspeople travel, frequently and often with little advance notice; (2) lagging preparation: families, travel, end-of-day fatigue, office homework, and other factors interfere with the necessary tasks of practice and preparation; (3) drift: in a long-term program, trainees often lose sight of the end goal, and motivation suffers; (4) wavering management support: managers may balk at devoting substantial portions of training budgets to a single program.

In 1982 we began to work with the ACTFL/ETS proficiency instruments. We immediately sensed that they offered a means of helping us address major questions of continuing program, course, and materials design as well as the four problem areas outlined above, especially the participants' sense of progress.

We also saw that the skill measurement system could be adapted to fit the company and that those refined standards could help us define needs more precisely. We could determine, with employee-trainees, what levels of skills their particular responsibilities require. We could establish clearer goals and thereby boost motivation.

As we began to work with the proficiency guidelines, we realized that they moved us toward the development of an adult educational (*andragogical*) model for foreign language instruction, which included another concept from adult education—the learning contract. The proficiency tools could assist us in specifying goals and objectives necessary for establishing the contract with the learner.

The following paragraphs summarize this theoretical context and discuss how performance contracting is being combined with proficiency concepts to develop an andragogical language training model which will not only meet individual needs but also fit changing organization contexts.

Conceptual basis in adult education

Theories of motivation abound, each postulating its own thesis of human nature and why people work in organizations. A history of theory regarding motivation is presented by Levinson in *The Great Jackass Fallacy* (10), and the concepts, based on insights from clinical work, which he presents in *Psychological Man* (9), offer a workable and, we believe, realistic understanding of motivation and work behavior. According to Levinson, the drive to achieve the ego ideal is the most powerful motivating factor in adults. The *ego ideal,* conditioned by parents, teachers, and other significant individuals and influences, is our picture of "how we should be at our ideal best." Achieving the ego ideal comes about as the adult closes the gap between the self-image and the ego ideal and results in greater self-esteem. Conversely, where there is no movement toward the ego ideal, there is no motivation, and self-esteem decreases.

Levinson also observes that a critical element in the adult personality in North American, and probably most, societies is the desire to see the self "as competent and effective in doing well what [one does]." Since self-esteem is a function of the discrepancy between ego esteem and self-image, it is important to be able to regard oneself as closely approximating the ego ideal (10, pp. 29–30).

Clearly this is a thumbnail sketch of a general, basic tendency, which at any time and/or in any individual can be conditioned by any number of internal or external factors, from the state of physical health to social roles and cultural norms. Yet the general pattern is observable in our history, culture, literature, and mythology. Consider, for example, the Protestant work ethic, which recent surveys and a new generation of college graduates show to be alive and well in America; Carl Sandberg's imagery of American drive and work energy; John Steinbeck's descriptions of middle American industrial might in *Travels with Charley;* and the legend of Paul Bunyan and Babe the Blue Ox, with its messages of power, accomplishment, and individual prowess.

Learning motivation in adults

This adult motivational profile, faced by any instructor in the adult classroom, brings us to the third consideration: what motivates adults to learn? Knowles (7) shows how this motivational profile enters the classroom, possibly much earlier than most assume, in his summation of the multiphase process of adult maturation. The implication for adult education lies in the conflict between individual andragogical motivation and the educational tradition of pedagogy in which the pupil/student role has been defined by concepts of childhood and youth, rather than by considerations of adulthood and increasing individual autonomy. Consequently, adults returning to the academic environment "have experienced culture shock in being treated as children" when confronted by the many policies, rules, and requirements characterizing the educational system. Knowles also stresses that development from childhood to adulthood, from dependence to autonomy, is a continuum, and that "children and youth are likely to be adult to some degree." Failure to perceive the extent to which individuals must be treated as adults engenders resentment, and the traditional education model fails to help adults achieve their ego ideals and therefore discourages motivation to learn (8, pp. 24–25).

Designing a model for adults

We have come to believe that our educational practice in the industrial classroom can benefit from a more rigorously andragogical approach. The steps in an andragogical system are: (1) the establishment of a climate conducive to adult learning; (2) the creation of an organizational structure for participative planning; (3) the diagnosis of needs for learning; (4) the formulation of directions of learning (objectives); (5) the development of a design of activities; (6) the operation of the activities; and (7) the rediagnosis of the needs for learning (evaluation) (8, p. 59).

We now examine our efforts from the perspective of the multiphase andragogical process. Several phases serve to illuminate aspects of our work and help place the function of the proficiency principles in business language programs—the prime focus of this article—into a more clearly defined relief. Using the andragogical process as an organizing principle also reflects the underlying structure of our efforts.

Steps one and two: Establishing a conducive climate and creating an orga-nizational structure. These apply primarily to start-up situations. In a five-year-old program, we have done what Knowles prescribes to the extent possible. He suggests rather elaborate and rigorous procedures for accomplishing these steps, prior to any training results. While we are constantly concerned with climate and structure, we have not had the luxury of working on them apart from showing training results.

Step three: Diagnosing needs. The proficiency guidelines measure *global* language proficiency and thus are not specific to any one organization or intended to measure mastery of specific job-related skills. However, re-placing the level-by-level linguistic behaviors of the global proficiency model with those of a specific organization, statements of precisely what an employee must be able to say, write, hear, read, and know at any level can be created for the organization. This produces a *subset* of global linguistic skills, which we call *performance criteria,* and their focused application in a specific context constitutes a nurturing of the proficiency concept's "hothouse special" (3, 5). Once criteria have been established, these proficiency and performance measurements become the means of defining skills required by jobs and of assessing the trainees' present capabilities.

This solves a vexing needs-analysis problem—our previous handicap in systematically describing the skills and levels to be achieved in our program. Learners enter the system with the awareness of a need, a lack: telexes are arriving from abroad and the manager must be able to compre-hend them. But how well? And what other reasons arise for use of the language? And at what level?

The needs-analysis process presupposes a precise, reliable, and valid method of acquiring needs data from managers and employees. In addi-tion to the proficiency guidelines, the trainer must know the organization and how to interview to obtain the information necessary for formulating workable company- and job-related criteria. For example, the trainer must be able to translate statements such as the following into definable skills and levels: "I need to be able to abstract technical articles." "I'd like to be fluent." "We need to prepare Sam for his two-year transfer to Germany." "I need to be able to follow along at meetings."

If we now have proficiency guidelines and performance criteria for our organization for all levels of all skills and cultural knowledge, we can begin to translate our telex recipient's need into instructional goals. She or he may well need to read telexes about transfers to an overseas branch at the Superior Level (ILR 3 and above). However, we may also discover that she or he has telephone exchanges with a bilingual secretary whose English needs repair. Therefore we will establish that our telex recipient needs Advanced-Level (ILR 2) knowledge of speaking, Superior (ILR 3) listen-ing skills, and no proficiency in writing.

The proficiency model provides the grid upon which to chart the skills and levels needed. When both our information and proficiency/performance interviews and tests are complete, we can formulate behaviorally specific guidelines for each learner's needs.

The proficiency tools and their adaptations do not, in reality, deal with the issues of the reliability of and commitment to the assessment. They cannot tell us whether other skills may be needed which the employee cannot or will not articulate, or whether the manager will continue to support the training. Therefore the needs assessment must include the views of both learner and manager. It must meet enough of the needs of manager, employee, and trainer to hold the commitment of all three partners.

Step four: Formulating learning objectives. When we record needs-analysis data using the proficiency guidelines and performance criteria, we have the basis for formulating learning objectives. For example, when we determine that a telex operator needs to speak at the Superior Level (ILR Level 3), listen at the Advanced Level, etc., we are setting learning objectives for that individual. Commitment is obtained by formalizing the statement of the objectives in the form of a learning or performance contract (7). The contract includes such information as what skills the job requires, long- and short-term levels to be achieved, means for measuring proficiency (global) and performance (job-specific), and the training plan.

Attempts to formulate contracts in the first year of our proficiency project have taught us the virtue of caution. At the outset a more general goal, obtaining general agreement on the need to pursue second language learning to the "end," is appropriate. The reason is simple: self-interest. Some managers balk at the idea of writing down on one document the skills and skill levels required by a job, measurement processes to be employed, restraints on publication of interview information, yearly achievement goals, long-range time goals, dollar commitments, etc. When discussing the use of a written contract, employees also shy away from the prospect of possible publication of evaluative material about their performance, regardless of guarantees of anonymity. Therefore caution and a measured, step-by-step approach are needed when using the proficiency and performance tools to determine objectives and commitments in a written contract.

Still, once the contract is obtained, it offers the benefits of commitment through mutually negotiated targets and measurability. The use of written contracts for language learning complements and completes the introduction of proficiency tools into the organizational language-learning process.

Step five: Developing a design of activities. Step five flows easily from this stage. The contracts and results of proficiency interviews provide an indication of which courses and tutorials to schedule. We know from our proficiency interviews and our needs discussions who needs to advance to a particular skills level. We also know from managers what additional needs may arise. A reading skills course, for example, resulted from information offered in a needs-analysis discussion with the company's chief operating officer. Thus the data we gather provides the basis for our yearly and long-term planning of offerings.

Step six: Operation of the activities. Proficiency guidelines, performance criteria, objectives, contracts, schedules, trainees, and instructors must then be transformed into a system of activities. We leave a thorough discussion of setting up comprehensive operations to Knowles (8). Our interest is more limited and lies in setting up operations for a foreign language learning program within a large organization, where the language program will usually be attached to the in-house Management Development function. This is the group responsible for ensuring that managers have the interpersonal, planning, and technical skills and policy/company culture knowledge to supervise and to do their jobs.

This type of structure means that some of the administrative duties often managed by a language professional are taken care of by others; but some of the freedom from administrative tasks is usurped by the increased number of roles played by the instructor. Many of these roles have little to do with proficiency, but all are required in order to maintain th training system.

We have been able to classify and adapt to new roles on the basis of the "Models for Excellence" study of the American Society for Training and Development (ASTD) (2). We believe that its findings apply to anyone doing training work in a noneducational institution, although the findings might apply to educational institutions as well.

The ASTD defines each training and development role in two ways: with a dictionary-type definition and with a list of the outputs of that role. The fifteen roles, identified in the ASTD publication, are:

- Evaluator
- Group Facilitator
- Individual Development Counselor
- Instructional Writer
- Instructor
- Manager of Training and Development
- Marketer
- Media Specialist
- Needs Analyst
- Program Administrator
- Program Designer
- Strategist
- Task Analyst

- Theoretician
- Transfer Agent.

In order to decide which roles applied to our experience, we simply checked off the outputs for which we have become responsible, role by role. A language trainer is obviously involved in roles such as evaluator, instructional writer, instructor, and program designer. But for only one role, that of individual development counselor, there were no outputs in our work to date—one exception in fifteen roles.

Managing a training system based on the proficiency guidelines and performance criteria propels the instructor into roles in which the tools themselves are not the prime concern. For example, in order to promote an awareness of foreign language skills needs and of the training programs, we have created virtually all outputs necessary for the role of marketer.

Step seven: Rediagnosis of learning needs. When learners entering the program have some prior language-learning background, proficiency and performance samples can help determine the skills retained by the learner and establish the starting point for training. Utilizing the proficiency guidelines in conjunction with performance criteria, learner progress can be monitored throughout the entire program of instruction, assessing the changing needs of the learner population and the organization. The performance criteria, especially, can provide the data from which to develop questions to test levels of need for a given job. Thus the proficiency tools and their adaptations also provide for follow-up and evaluation.

Conclusions and Implications: Proficiency and Business

Clearly, operating an in-house adult second language learning system is a challenging managerial effort. Proficiency concepts and andragogical process are inseparable in organizations of working adults where language or other skills training is done. Adults respond best to a learning environment that moves them toward their goals. We have observed this in our language and management development efforts and have responded by providing an andragogical basis for our programs. Applications of the proficiency guidelines, initially implemented as a separate project, proved to parallel most phases of the andragogical process.

For our optimal benefit, the performance criteria, tailored to business and industry and to the company, had to be added to the system. We have to teach business-related, company-specific content in order to provide a useful service to our learners; therefore, we need to measure the impact of both global and focused skills training. Even before we began the tailoring process, we believed the proficiency concepts would enable us to: (1) assess needs more precisely, (2) define objectives behaviorally and gain commitment from the organization by means of performance contracts, (3) gather data for program and materials design, (4) measure impact at the individual level more effectively, (5) increase participation in the learning design, and (6) clarify the participants' sense of progress.

Symbiosis in Academic, Government, and Industry Proficiency Efforts

There can be no doubt that many adults, not only those within the business/industrial and government communities, *want* foreign language skills. There is also no doubt that adults *need* these skills. Whether it be for job purposes, professional advancement, personal enrichment, travel, family heritage or myriad other reasons, the long-standing and continuing popularity of language offerings in adult education curricula and in private language schools across the country attests to the existence of foreign language learning needs beyond the years of formal education.

Our main focus has been a business/industrial context, for purposes of illustrating major points, and because this context represents a large, important clientele with requirements both different from and similar to that other major field of job-related adult foreign language training, the government.

It is clear that government, industry, and the professions have a need for personnel with foreign language proficiency, proficiency which can be put to immediate and specific use. And while each branch of government service, each corporation, each job, and each profession has its own particular requirements and while some level of on-the-job training may always be necessary, much of the type of training currently conducted by and for government and industry would be superfluous *if students were leaving the educational system with functional skills.*

The government, through the ILR definitions, and the academic community, through the ACTFL guidelines, are providing the tools with which to begin defining, measuring, and assuring proficiency. As efforts within the academic community become increasingly effective, government, business, and the professions will profit from the improved foreign language proficiency levels achieved. The tasks of language trainers for government, business, and the professions can then become what will benefit those sectors most: more tailored, more focused, more effective in less time. The foundation upon which their efforts can build will have been established.

A substantial part of the need for our effort derives from the fact that most Americans have no functional foreign language proficiency. We are fortunate to work with a generous and open-minded company: most would simply not fund such an extensive effort. Therefore, it is important to create a situation in which foreign language training for the workplace becomes simultaneously more productive and less demanding. Many foreign nationals are able to begin work in the United States after a month's intensive polishing of their English and a few months of weekly individual tutoring in pronunciation and idiom. The same cannot be said of their American colleagues; that is our *raison d'être*. Yet a company will more readily support the former form of quick, low visibility effort than a highly visible one which demands literally years of effort and a considerable budget. The more functional language skills that students have upon graduation, the more effectively and efficiently we will be able to do our job and the more worthwhile any subsequent investment will be to the organization and the better prepared the graduate, the better and more varied the opportunities in the "outside" world.

The increase in courses now focusing on such areas as business, social services, etc., offers students a *broad contextual foreign language background* upon which instruction can build later. We should strive for such *breadth of exposure* as an inherent part of basic secondary and higher education. Our experience in "alternative" careers has shown that familiarity with economics and the contemporary business organization is significant, and we urge inclusion of such topics in general studies curricula.

The ILR definitions, the ACTFL guidelines, and their subsequent adaptations and applications will help those working outside the academic community to define the foreign language needs (type of skill, function, content, and accuracy levels) which exist "outside." Improved articulation of these needs will help those within the educational community refine courses and materials, ensuring the best possible academic preparation.

The academic community can profit in turn from the expertise of their colleagues on the "outside," their experience in methodology and in curriculum and materials design, and from the andragogical and highly applications-oriented perspectives of the training environment. Especially college and university faculty should be aware of the implications of andragogy, since their students are surely at the threshold of adult learning. Many have identified majors or areas of study in which they have a career interest and thus are not far removed from those needing on-the-job training. And with the shift in academic populations toward more adult learners, the working adult already represents an increasing percentage of the student population.

The proficiency concepts, applied in the context of andragogy, allow us to facilitate the learning process as it must largely be defined, understood, and accepted by the learner; thus it allows us to consult with the learner about needs, short- and long-term goals, methods, and materials; to help plan and manage, from our critically important professional perspective, the individual's learning process. Proficiency concepts help the student—once aware of the system, its goals, and the nature of the language learning process—to communicate individual goals more accurately and effectively, to better inform our planning and design.

"Traditional" full-time, nonworking students, at least, have a tremendous advantage in the time available to learn a language prior to the need for skills. They also have the advantage of studying at a time when foreign language educators are attempting to meet a broader range of career and professional needs. Finally, all students have the advantage of studying at a time when both educators and the marketplace are becoming aware of the proficiency tools and are in a position to apply them to program and materials design.

Although the many roles played by language professionals in business and industry are often not readily perceived as being part and parcel of the academic language professional's everyday responsibilities, there are significant advantages to incorporating these roles more consciously into the academic branch of the profession. We have, in the wake of the "Great Enrollments Depression," become keenly aware of how critical the marketing function has become in the academic context.

For the first time in a long time, it appears that the language teaching profession verges on the development of a skills-based system which will not only enhance the articulation of instruction within the entire educational system but also can be the Esperanto enabling articulation of the process between the educational system and the "outside" worlds of government, industry, and the professions. At the same time, it allows articulation between individual learner and teacher-facilitator of what the common endeavor is to be.

It is an exciting time in language teaching. No less so out here.

References, Proficiency beyond the Academic Classroom

1. *ACTFL Provisional Proficiency Guidelines.* Hastings-on-Hudson, NY: American Council on the Teaching of Foreign Languages, 1982.
2. American Society for Training and Development. "Models for Excellence: The Conclusions and Recommendations of the ASTD Training and Development Competency Study." Washington, DC: American Society for Training and Development, 1983.
3. Buck, Kathryn. "Nurturing the Hothouse Special: When Proficiency Becomes Performance." *Die Unterrichtspraxis* 17, 2 (Fall 1984): forthcoming.
4. _____, and Warren Born. *Options for the Teaching of Foreign Languages, Literatures, and Cultures.* New York: American Council on the Teaching of Foreign Languages, 1978.
5. _____, and Pardee Lowe, Jr. *Provisional Business Foreign Language Performance Criteria.* Forthcoming.
6. Hiple, David V., and Kathryn Buck. "The Rationale for Defining and Measuring Foreign Language Proficiency in Programs for Business." *Foreign Language Annals,* forthcoming.
7. Knowles, Malcolm S. *The Adult Learner: A Neglected Species.* Houston, TX: Gulf Publishing Co., 1978.

8. _____. *The Modern Practice of Adult Education: From Pedagogy to Andragogy.* New York: Cambridge, The Adult Education Company, 1980.
9. Levinson, Harry. *Psychological Man.* Cambridge, MA: The Levinson Institute, 1976.
10. _____. *The Great Jackass Fallacy.* Boston, MA: Harvard University Division of Research, Graduate School of Business Administration, 1973.
11. Simon, Paul. *The Tongue-Tied American: Confronting the Foreign Language Crisis.* New York: Continuum, 1980.

Appendix A:
The ACTFL Provisional Proficiency Guidelines

Provisional Generic Descriptions—Speaking

Novice—Low Unable to function in the spoken language. Oral production is limited to occasional isolated words. Essentially no communicative ability.

Novice—Mid Able to operate only in a very limited capacity within very predictable areas of need. Vocabulary limited to that necessary to express simple elementary needs and basic courtesy formulae. Syntax is fragmented, inflections and word endings frequently omitted, confused or distorted and the majority of utterances consist of isolated words or short formulae. Utterances rarely consist of more than two or three words and are marked by frequent long pauses and repetition of an interlocutor's words. Pronunciation is frequently unintelligible and is strongly influenced by first language. Can be understood only with difficulty, even by persons such as teachers who are used to speaking with nonnative speakers or in interactions where the context strongly supports the utterance.

Novice—High Able to satisfy immediate needs using learned utterances. Can ask questions or make statements with reasonable accuracy only where this involves short memorized utterances or formulae. There is no real autonomy of expression, although there may be some emerging signs of spontaneity and flexibility. There is a slight increase in utterance length but frequent long pauses and repetition of interlocutor's words still occur. Most utterances are telegraphic and word endings are often omitted, confused, or distorted. Vocabulary is limited to areas of immediate survival needs. Can differentiate most phonemes when produced in isolation but when they are combined in words or groups of words, errors are frequent and, even with repetition, may severely inhibit communication even with persons used to dealing with such learners. Little development in stress and intonation is evident.

Intermediate—Low Able to satisfy basic survival needs and minimum courtesy requirements. In areas of immediate need or on very familiar topics, can ask and answer simple questions, initiate and respond to simple statements, and maintain very simple face-to-face conversations. When asked to do so, is able to formulate some questions with limited constructions and much inaccuracy. Almost every utterance contains fractured syntax and other grammatical errors. Vocabulary inadequate to express anything but the most elementary needs. Strong interference from native language occurs in articulation, stress, and intonation. Misunderstandings frequently arise from limited vocabulary and grammar and erroneous phonology but, with repetition, can generally be understood by native speakers in regular contact with foreigners attempting to speak their language. Little precision in information conveyed owing to tentative state of grammatical development and little or no use of modifiers.

Intermediate—Mid Able to satisfy some survival needs and some limited social demands. Is able to formulate some questions when asked to do so. Vocabulary permits discussion of topics beyond basic survival needs such as personal history and leisure-time activities. Some evidence of grammatical accuracy in basic constructions, for example, subject-verb agreement, noun-adjective agreement, some notion of inflection.

Intermediate—High   Able to satisfy most survival needs and limited social demands. Shows some spontaneity in language production but fluency is very uneven. Can initiate and sustain a general conversation but has little understanding of the social conventions of conversation. Developing flexibility in a range of circumstances beyond immediate survival needs. Limited vocabulary range necessitates much hesitation and circumlocution. The commoner tense forms occur but errors are frequent in formation and selection. Can use most question forms. While some word order is established, errors still occur in more complex patterns. Cannot sustain coherent structures in longer utterances or unfamiliar situations. Ability to describe and give precise information is limited. Aware of basic cohesive features such as pronouns and verb inflections, but many are unreliable, especially if less immediate in reference. Extended discourse is largely a series of short, discrete utterances. Articulation is comprehensible to native speakers used to dealing with foreigners, and can combine most phonemes with reasonable comprehensibility, but still has difficulty in producing certain sounds, in certain positions, or in certain combinations, and speech will usually be labored. Still has to repeat utterances frequently to be understood by the general public. Able to produce some narration in either past or future.

Advanced   Able to satisfy routine social demands and limited work requirements. Can handle with confidence but not with facility most social situations including introductions and casual conversations about current events, as well as work, family, and autobiographical information; can handle limited work requirements, needing help in handling any complications or difficulties. Has a speaking vocabulary sufficient to respond simply with some circumlocutions; accent, though often quite faulty, is intelligible; can usually handle elementary constructions quite accurately but does not have thorough or confident control of the grammar.

Advanced Plus   Able to satisfy most work requirements and show some ability to communicate on concrete topics relating to particular interests and special fields of competence. Generally strong in either grammar or vocabulary, but not in both. Weaknesses or unevenness in one of the foregoing or in pronunciation result in occasional miscommunication. Areas of weakness range from simple constructions such as plurals, articles, prepositions, and negatives to more complex structures such as tense usage, passive constructions, word order, and relative clauses. Normally controls general vocabulary with some groping for everyday vocabulary still evident. Often shows remarkable fluency and ease of speech, but under tension or pressure language may break down.

Superior   Able to speak the language with sufficient structural accuracy and vocabulary to participate effectively in most formal and informal conversations on practical, social, and professional topics. Can discuss particular interests and special fields of competence with reasonable ease. Vocabulary is broad enough that speaker rarely has to grope for a word; accent may be obviously foreign; control of grammar good; errors virtually never interfere with understanding and rarely disturb the native speaker.

Provisional Generic Descriptions—Listening

Novice—Low   No practical understanding of the spoken language. Understanding limited to occasional isolated words, such as cognates, borrowed words, and high-frequency social conventions. Essentially no ability to comprehend even short utterances.

Novice—Mid   Sufficient comprehension to understand some memorized words within predictable areas of need. Vocabulary for comprehension limited to simple elementary needs and basic courtesy formulae. Utterances understood rarely exceed more than two or three words at a time and ability to understand is characterized by long pauses for assimilation and by repeated requests on the listener's part for repetition and/or a slower rate of speech. Confuses words that sound similar.

Novice—High Sufficient comprehension to understand a number of memorized utterances in areas of immediate need. Comprehends slightly longer utterances in situations where the context aids understanding, such as at the table, in a restaurant/store, in a train/bus. Phrases recognized have for the most part been memorized. Comprehends vocabulary common to daily needs. Comprehends simple questions/statements about family members, age, address, weather, time, daily activities, and interests. Misunderstandings arise from failure to perceive critical sounds or endings. Understands even standard speech with difficulty but gets some main ideas. Often requires repetition and/or a slowed rate of speed for comprehension, even when listening to persons such as teachers who are used to speaking with nonnatives.

Intermediate—Low Sufficient comprehension to understand utterances about basic survival needs, minimum courtesy, and travel requirements. In areas of immediate need or on very familiar topics, can understand nonmemorized material, such as simple questions and answers, statements, and face-to-face conversations in the standard language. Comprehension areas include basic needs: meals, lodging, transportation, time, simple instructions (e.g., route directions), and routine commands (e.g., from customs officials, police). Understands main ideas. Misunderstandings frequently arise from lack of vocabulary or faulty processing of syntactic information often caused by strong interference from the native language or by the imperfect and partial acquisition of the target grammar.

Intermediate—Mid Sufficient comprehension to understand simple conversations about some survival needs and some limited social conventions. Vocabulary permits understanding of topics beyond basic survival needs such as personal history and leisure-time activities. Evidence of understanding basic constructions, for example, subject-verb agreement, noun-adjective agreement; evidence that some inflection is understood.

Intermediate—High Sufficient comprehension to understand short conversations about most survival needs and limited social conventions. Increasingly able to understand topics beyond immediate survival needs. Shows spontaneity in understanding, but speed and consistency of understanding uneven. Limited vocabulary range necessitates repetition for understanding. Understands commoner tense forms and some word order patterns, including most question forms, but miscommunication still occurs with more complex patterns. Can get the gist of conversations, but cannot sustain comprehension in longer utterances or in unfamiliar situations. Understanding of descriptions and detailed information is limited. Aware of basic cohesive features such as pronouns and verb inflections, but many are unreliably understood, especially if other material intervenes. Understanding is largely limited to a series of short, discrete utterances. Still has to ask for utterances to be repeated. Some ability to understand the facts.

Advanced Sufficient comprehension to understand conversations about routine social conventions and limited school or work requirements. Able to understand face-to-face speech in the standard language, delivered at a normal rate with some repetition and rewording by a native speaker not used to dealing with foreigners. Understands everyday topics, common personal and family news, well-known current events, and routine matters involving school or work; descriptions and narration about current, past and future events; and essential points of discussion or speech at an elementary level on topics in special fields of interest.

Advanced Plus Sufficient comprehension to understand most routine social conventions, conversations on school or work requirements, and discussions on concrete topics related to particular interests and special fields of competence. Often shows remarkable ability and ease of understanding, but comprehension may break down under tension or pressure, including unfavorable listening conditions. Candidate may display weakness or deficiency due to inadequate vocabulary base or less than secure knowledge of grammar and syntax. Normally understands general vocabulary with some hesitant understanding of everyday vocabulary still evident. Can sometimes detect emotional overtones. Some ability to understand between the lines, i.e., to make inferences.

Superior   Sufficient comprehension to understand the essentials of all speech in standard dialects, including technical discussions within a special field. Has sufficient understanding of face-to-face speech, delivered with normal clarity and speed in standard language on general topics and areas of special interest; understands hypothesizing and supported opinions. Has broad enough vocabulary that rarely has to ask for paraphrasing or explanation. Can follow accurately the essentials of conversations between educated native speakers, reasonably clear telephone calls, radio broadcasts, standard news items, oral reports, some oral technical reports, and public addresses on nontechnical subjects. May not understand native speakers if they speak very quickly or use some slang or unfamiliar dialect. Can often detect emotional overtones. Can understand "between the lines" (i.e., make inferences).

Provisional Generic Descriptions—Reading

Novice—Low   No functional ability in reading the foreign language.

Novice—Mid   Sufficient understanding of the written language to interpret highly contextualized words or cognates within predictable areas. Vocabulary for comprehension limited to simple elementary needs such as names, addresses, dates, street signs, building names, short informative signs (e.g., no smoking, entrance/exit), and formulaic vocabulary requesting same. Material understood rarely exceeds a single phrase and comprehension requires successive rereading and checking.

Novice—High   Sufficient comprehension of the written language to interpret set expressions in areas of immediate need. Can recognize all the letters in the printed version of an alphabetic system and high-frequency elements of a syllabary or a character system. Where vocabulary has been mastered, can read for instruction and directional purposes standardized messages, phrases, or expressions such as some items on menus, schedules, timetables, maps, and signs indicating hours of operation, social codes, and traffic regulations. This material is read only for essential information. Detail is overlooked or misunderstood.

Intermediate—Low   Sufficient comprehension to understand in printed form the simplest connected material, either authentic or specially prepared, dealing with basic survival and social needs. Able to understand both mastered material and recombinations of the mastered elements that achieve meanings at the same level. Understands main ideas in material whose structures and syntax parallel the native language. Can read messages, greetings, statements of social amenities or other simple language containing only the highest frequency grammatical patterns and vocabulary items including cognates (if appropriate). Misunderstandings arise when syntax diverges from that of the native language or when grammatical cues are overlooked.

Intermediate—Mid   Sufficient comprehension to understand in printed form simple discourse for informative or social purposes. In response to perceived needs, can read for information material such as announcements of public events, popular advertising, notes containing biographical information or narration of events, and straightforward newspaper headlines and story titles. Can guess at unfamiliar vocabulary if highly contextualized. Relies primarily on adverbs as time indicators. Has some difficulty with the cohesive factors in discourse, such as matching pronouns with referents. May have to read material several times before understanding.

Intermediate—High   Sufficient comprehension to understand a simple paragraph for personal communication, information, or recreational purposes. Can read with understanding social notes, letters, and invitations; can locate and derive main ideas of the introductory/summary paragraphs from high interest or familiar news or other informational sources; can read for pleasure specially prepared, or some uncomplicated authentic prose, such as fictional narratives or cultural information. Shows spontaneity in reading by ability to guess at meaning from context. Understands common time indicators and can interpret some cohesive factors such as objective pronouns and simple clause connectors. Begins to relate sentences in the discourse to advance meaning but cannot sustain understanding of longer discourse on unfamiliar topics. Misinterpretation still occurs with more complex patterns.

Advanced Sufficient comprehension to read simple authentic printed material or edited textual material within a familiar context. Can read uncomplicated but authentic prose on familiar subjects containing description and narration such as news items describing frequently occurring events, simple biographic information, social notices, and standard business letters. Can read edited texts such as prose fiction and contemporary culture. The prose is predominantly in familiar sentence patterns. Can follow essential points of written discussion at level of main ideas and some supporting ones with topics in a field of interest or where background exists. Some misunderstandings. Able to read the facts but cannot draw inferences.

Advanced Plus Sufficient comprehension to understand most factual information in non-technical prose as well as some discussions on concrete topics related to special interests. Able to read for information and description, to follow sequence of events, and to react to that information. Is able to separate main ideas from lesser ones, and uses that division to advance understanding. Can locate and interpret main ideas and details in material written for the general public. Will begin to guess sensibly at new words by using linguistic context and prior knowledge. May react personally to material but does not yet detect subjective attitudes, values, or judgments in the writing.

Superior Able to read standard newspaper items addressed to the general reader, routine correspondence reports and technical material in a field of interest at a normal rate of speed (at least 220 wpm). Readers can gain new knowledge from material on unfamiliar topics in areas of a general nature. Can interpret hypotheses, supported opinions, and conjectures. Can also read short stories, novels, and other recreational literature accessible to the general public. Reading ability is not subject-matter dependent. Has broad enough general vocabulary that successful guessing resolves problems with complex structures and low-frequency idioms. Misreading is rare. Almost always produces correct interpretation. Able to read between the lines. May be unable to appreciate nuance or stylistics.

Provisional Generic Descriptions—Writing

Novice—Low No functional ability in writing the foreign language.

Novice—Mid No practical communicative writing skills. Able to copy isolated words or short phrases. Able to transcribe previously studied words or phrases.

Novice—High Able to write simple fixed expressions and limited memorized material. Can supply information when requested on forms such as hotel registrations and travel documents. Can write names, numbers, dates, one's own nationality, addresses, and other simple biographic information, as well as learned vocabulary, short phrases, and simple lists. Can write all the symbols in an alphabetic or syllabic system or 50 of the most common characters. Can write simple memorized material with frequent misspellings and inaccuracies.

Intermediate—Low Has sufficient control of the writing system to meet limited practical needs. Can write short messages, such as simple questions or notes, postcards, phone messages, and the like within the scope of limited language experience. Can take simple notes on material dealing with very familiar topics, although memory span is extremely limited. Can create statements or questions within the scope of limited language experience. Material produced consists of recombinations of learned vocabulary and structures into simple sentences. Vocabulary is inadequate to express anything but elementary needs. Writing tends to be a loosely organized collection of sentence fragments on a very familiar topic. Makes continual errors in spelling, grammar, and punctuation, but writing can be read and understood by a native speaker used to dealing with foreigners. Able to produce appropriately some fundamental sociolinguistic distinctions in formal and familiar style, such as appropriate subject pronouns, titles of address, and basic social formulae.

Intermediate—Mid   Sufficient control of writing system to meet some survival needs and some limited social demands. Able to compose short paragraphs or take simple notes on very familiar topics grounded in personal experience. Can discuss likes and dislikes, daily routine, everyday events, and the like. Can express past time, using content words and time expressions, or with sporadically accurate verbs. Evidence of good control of basic constructions and inflections such as subject-verb agreement, noun-adjective agreement, and straightforward syntactic constructions in present or future time, though errors occasionally occur. May make frequent errors, however, when venturing beyond current level of linguistic competence. When resorting to a dictionary, often is unable to identify appropriate vocabulary, or uses dictionary entry in uninflected form.

Intermediate—High   Sufficient control of writing system to meet most survival needs and limited social demands. Can take notes in some detail on familiar topics, and respond to personal questions using elementary vocabulary and common structures. Can write simple letters, brief synopses and paraphrases, summaries of biographical data and work experience, and short compositions on familiar topics. Can create sentences and short paragraphs relating to most survival needs (food, lodging, transportation, immediate surroundings, and situations) and limited social demands. Can relate personal history, discuss topics such as daily life, preferences, and other familiar material. Can express fairly accurately present and future time. Can produce some past verb forms, but not always accurately or with correct usage. Shows good control of elementary vocabulary and some control of basic syntactic patterns but major errors still occur when expressing more complex thoughts. Dictionary usage may still yield incorrect vocabulary of forms, although can use a dictionary to advantage to express simple ideas. Generally cannot use basic cohesive elements of discourse to advantage such as relative constructions, subject pronouns, connectors, etc. Writing, though faulty, is comprehensible to native speakers used to dealing with foreigners.

Advanced   Able to write routine correspondence and simple discourse of at least several paragraphs on familiar topics. Can write simple social correspondence, take notes, and write cohesive summaries, résumés, and short narratives and descriptions on factual topics. Able to write about everyday topics using both description and narration. Has sufficient writing vocabulary to express himself/herself simply with some circumlocution. Can write about a very limited number of current events or daily situations and express personal preferences and observations in some detail, using basic structures. Still makes common errors in spelling and punctuation, but shows some control of the most common formats and punctuation conventions. Good control of the morphology of the language (in inflected languages) and of the most frequently used syntactic structures. Elementary constructions are usually handled quite accurately, and writing is understandable to a native speaker not used to reading the writing of foreigners. Uses a limited number of cohesive devices such as pronouns and repeated words with good accuracy. Able to join sentences in limited discourse, but has difficulty and makes frequent errors in producing complex sentences. Paragraphs are reasonably unified and coherent.

Advanced Plus Shows ability to write about most common topics with some precision and in some detail. Can write fairly detailed résumés and summaries and take quite accurate notes. Can write most social and informal business correspondence. Can describe and narrate personal experiences and explain simply points of view in prose discourse. Can write about concrete topics relating to particular interests and special fields of competence. Normally controls general vocabulary with some circumlocution. Often shows remarkable fluency and ease of expression, but under time constraints and pressure, language may be inaccurate and/or incomprehensible. Generally strong in either grammar or vocabulary, but not in both. Weaknesses and unevenness in one of the foregoing or in spelling result in occasional miscommunication. Areas of weakness range from simple constructions such as plurals, articles, prepositions, and negatives to more complex structures such as tense usage, passive constructions, word order, and relative clauses. Some misuse of vocabulary still evident. Shows a limited ability to use circumlocution. Uses dictionary to advantage to supply unknown words. Writing is understandable to native speakers not used to reading material written by nonnatives, though the style is still obviously foreign.

Superior Able to use the written language effectively in most formal and informal exchanges on practical, social, and professional topics. Can write most types of correspondence, such as memos and social and business letters, short research papers, and statements of position in areas of special interest or in special fields. Can express hypotheses, conjectures, and present arguments or points of view accurately and effectively. Can write about areas of special interest and handle topics in special fields, in addition to most common topics. Good control of a full range of structures, spelling, and a wide general vocabulary allow the writer to convey his/her message accurately, though style may be foreign. Can use complex and compound sentence structures to express ideas clearly and coherently. Uses dictionary with a high degree of accuracy to supply specialized vocabulary. Errors, though sometimes made when using more complex structures, are occasional, and rarely disturb the native speaker. Sporadic errors when using basic structures. Although sensitive to differences in formal and informal style, still cannot tailor writing precisely and accurately to a variety of audiences or styles.

Provisional Generic Descriptions—Culture

Novice Limited interaction. Behaves with considerateness. Is resourceful in nonverbal communication, but is unreliable in interpretation of nonverbal cues. Is limited in language, as indicated under the listening and speaking skills. Lacks generally the knowledge of culture patterns requisite for survival situations.

Intermediate Survival competence. Can deal with familiar survival situations and interact with a culture bearer accustomed to foreigners. Uses behavior acquired for the purpose of greeting and leave-taking, expressing wants, asking directions, buying food, using transportation, tipping. Comprehends the response. Makes errors as the result of misunderstanding; miscommunicates, and misapplies assumptions about the culture.

Advanced Limited social competence. Handles routine social situations successfully with a culture bearer accustomed to foreigners. Shows comprehension of common rules of etiquette, taboos, and sensitivities, though home culture predominates. Can make polite requests, accept and refuse invitations, offer and receive gifts, apologize, make introductions, telephone, purchase and bargain, do routine banking. Can discuss a few aspects of the home and the foreign country, such as general current events and policies, as well as a field of personal interest. Does not offend the culture bearer, but some important misunderstandings and miscommunications occur in interaction with one unaccustomed to foreigners. Is not competent to take part in a formal meeting or in a group situation where several persons are speaking informally at the same time.

Superior Working social and professional competence. Can participate in almost all social situations and those within one vocation. Handles unfamiliar types of situations with ease and sensitivity, including some involving common taboos, or other emotionally charged subjects. Comprehends most nonverbal responses. Laughs at some culture-related humor. In productive skills, neither culture predominates; nevertheless, makes appropriate use of cultural references and expressions. Generally distinguishes between a formal and informal register. Discusses abstract ideas relating the foreign to the native culture. Is generally limited, however, in handling abstractions. Minor inaccuracies occur in perception of meaning and in the expression of the intended representation but do not result in serious misunderstanding, even by a culture bearer unaccustomed to foreigners.

Near-Native Competence Full social and professional competence. Fits behavior to audience, and the culture of the target language dominates almost entirely. Has internalized the concept that culture is relative and is always on the lookout to do the appropriate thing. Can counsel, persuade, negotiate, represent a point of view, interpret for dignitaries, describe and compare features of the two cultures. In such comparisons, can discuss geography, history, institutions, customs and behavior patterns, current events, and national policies. Perceives almost all unverbalized responses, and recognizes almost all allusions, including historical and literary commonplaces. Laughs at most culture-related humor. Controls a formal and informal register of behavior. Is inferior to the culture bearer only in background information related to the culture such as childhood experiences, detailed regional geography, and past events of significance.

Native Competence Examinee is indistinguishable from a person brought up and educated in the culture.

ACTFL would like to thank the following educators who worked so diligently to create these guidelines:

Sabine Atwell	Gail Guntermann	Nina Levinson	June K. Phillips*
Jeannette D. Bragger	Charles R. Hancock	Judith E. Liskin-Gasparro*	Micheline Ponder
Raymonde Brown	Juana A. Hernández	Helene Z. Loew	Claus Reschke
Kathryn Buck	Theodore V. Higgs	Pardee Lowe, Jr.*	Jean-Charles Seigneuret
James Child	Nancy A. Humbach	Frankie McCullough	Dagmar Waters
Ray T. Clifford	Joseph Labat	Howard L. Nostrand	Eugene Weber
Barbara F. Freed	Dale L. Lange*	Alice C. Omaggio*	

*Language Coordinator

Appendix B:
Interagency Language Roundtable
Level Definitions

Elementary Proficiency (S-1) *Able to satisfy routine travel needs and minimum courtesy requirements.* Can ask and answer questions on very familiar topics; within the scope of very limited language experience, can understand simple questions and statements, allowing for slowed speech, repetition or paraphrase; speaking vocabulary inadequate to express anything but the most elementary needs; errors in pronunciation and grammar are frequent, but can be understood by a native speaker used to dealing with foreigners attempting to speak the language; while topics which are "very familiar" and elementary needs vary considerably from individual to individual, any person at the S-1 level should be able to order a simple meal, ask for shelter or lodging, ask and give simple directions, make purchases, and tell time.

Limited Working Proficiency (S-2) *Able to satisfy routine social demands and limited work requirements.* Can handle with confidence but not with facility most social situations including introductions and casual conversations about current events, as well as work, family, and autobiographical information; can handle limited work requirements, needing help in handling any complications or difficulties; can get the gist of most conversations on nontechnical subjects (i.e., topics which require no specialized knowledge), and has a speaking vocabulary sufficient to respond simply with some circumlocutions; accent, though often quite faulty, is intelligible; can usually handle elementary constructions quite accurately but does not have thorough or confident control of the grammar.

Professional Working Proficiency (S-3) *Able to speak the language with sufficient structural accuracy and vocabulary to participate effectively in most formal and informal conversations on practical, social, and professional topics.* Can discuss particular interests and special fields of competence with reasonable ease; comprehension is quite complete for a normal rate of speech; general vocabulary is broad enough that he or she rarely has to grope for a word; accent may be obviously foreign; control of grammar good; errors virtually never interfere with understanding and rarely disturb the native speaker.

Full Professional Proficiency (S-4) *Able to use the language fluently and accurately on all levels normally pertinent to professional needs.* Can understand and participate in any conversation within the range of own personal and professional experience with a high degree of fluency and precision of vocabulary; would rarely be taken for a native speaker, but can respond appropriately even in unfamiliar situations; errors of pronunciation and grammar quite rare and unpatterned; can handle informal interpreting from and into the language.

Native or Bilingual Proficiency (S-5) *Speaking proficiency equivalent to that of an educated native speaker.* Has complete fluency in the language such that speech on all levels is fully accepted by ENS in all of its features, including breadth of vocabulary and idiom, colloquialisms, and pertinent cultural references.

Index to
Persons Cited

Index to Topics
and Institutions Cited

Central States Conference Proceedings

Published annually in conjunction with the
Central States Conference on the Teaching of Foreign Languages

Proficiency, Policy, and Professionalism in Foreign Language
Education
ed. Birckbichler (1987)

Second Language Acquisition: Preparing for Tomorrow
ed. Snyder (1986)

Meeting the call for Excellence in the Foreign Language Classroom
ed. Westphal (1985)

Strategies for Foreign Language Teaching:
Communication • Technology • Culture
ed. Westphal (1984)

The Foreign Language Classroom: New Techniques
ed. Garfinkel (1983)

ESL and the Foreign Language Teacher
ed. Garfinkel (1982)

A Global Approach to Foreign Language Education
ed. Conner (1981)

New Frontiers in Foreign Language Education
ed. Conner (1980)

Teaching the Basics in the Foreign Language Classroom
ed. Benseler (1979)

Teaching for Tomorrow in the Foreign Language Classroom
ed. Baker (1978)

Personalizing Foreign Language Instruction:
Learning Styles and Teaching Options
ed. Schulz (1977)

Teaching for Communication in the Foreign Language Classroom
ed. Schulz (1976)

The Culture Revolution in Foreign Language Teaching
ed. Lafayette (1975)

Careers, Communication & Culture in Foreign Language Teaching
ed. Grittner (1974)

For further information or a current catalog, write:
National Textbook Company
4255 West Touhy Avenue
Lincolnwood, Illinois 60646-1975 U.S.A.

NTC PROFESSIONAL MATERIALS

ACTFL Review

Published annually in conjunction with the American Council on the Teaching of Foreign Languages

Modern Media in Foreign Language Education: Theory and Implementation, *ed. Smith*, Vol. 18 (1987)

Defining and Developing Proficiency: Guidelines, Implementations, and Concepts, *ed. Byrnes*, Vol. 17 (1986)

Foreign Language Proficiency in the Classroom and Beyond, *ed. James*, Vol. 16 (1984)

Teaching for Proficiency, the Organizing Principle, *ed. Higgs*, Vol. 15 (1983)

Practical Applications of Research in Foreign Language Teaching, *ed. James*, Vol. 14 (1982)

Curriculum, Competence, and the Foreign Language Teacher, *ed. Higgs*, Vol. 13 (1981)

Action for the '80s: A Political, Professional, and Public Program for Foreign Language Education, *ed. Phillips*, Vol. 12 (1980)

The New Imperative: Expanding the Horizons of Foreign Language Education, *ed. Phillips*, Vol. 11 (1979)

Building on Experience—Building for Success, *ed. Phillips*, Vol. 10 (1978)

The Language Connection: From the Classroom to the World, *ed. Phillips*, Vol. 9 (1977)

An Integrative Approach to Foreign Language Teaching: Choosing Among the Options, *eds. Jarvis and Omaggio*, Vol. 8 (1976)

Perspective: A New Freedom, *ed. Jarvis*, Vol. 7 (1975)

The Challenge of Communication, *ed. Jarvis*, Vol. 6 (1974)

Foreign Language Education: A Reappraisal, *eds. Lange and James*, Vol. 4 (1972)

Foreign Language Education: An Overview, *ed. Birkmaier*, Vol. 1 (1969)

Professional Resources

Complete Guide to Exploratory Foreign Language Programs, *Kennedy and de Lorenzo*

Award-Winning Foreign Language Programs: Prescriptions for Success, *Sims and Hammond*

Living in Latin America: A Case Study in Cross-Cultural Communication, *Gorden*

Teaching Culture: Strategies for Intercultural Communication, *Seelye*

Individualized Foreign Language Instruction, *Grittner and LaLeike*

Oral Communication Testing, *Linder*

Transcription and Transliteration, *Wellisch*

ABC's of Languages and Linguistics

A TESOL Professional Anthology: Grammar and Composition

A TESOL Professional Anthology: Listening, Speaking, and Reading

A TESOL Professional Anthology: Culture

For further information or a current catalog, write:
National Textbook Company
4255 West Touhy Avenue
Lincolnwood, Illinois 60646-1975 U.S.A.